herstory

migration stories of African women in Ireland

Published by AkiDwA African Womens Network
Copyright © 2006 AkiDwA
9c Lower Abbey Street, Dublin, Ireland

ISBN-10: 0-9552275-0-X
ISBN-13: 978-0-9552275-0-9

This publication contains a collection of testimonies from African women of various
countries that migrated to Ireland under different circumstances. The names of the
women have been changed to protect their anonymity. The testimonies have been
collected by Pamela Akinjobi on behalf of AkiDwA. AkiDwA cannot accept
responsibility for the factual accuracy of information presented by individual women
nor for the representation of this information by Ms. Akinjobi.

Design by Public Communications Centre

Dedication

AkiDwA would like to dedicate this book to all daughters, sisters, wives and
mothers of Africa. May you all receive the strength you need to fulfil.

Also, to African women all over the world especially in Ireland.
To those of you who had the courage to share your stories,
this is to you for never giving up the struggle against the
storms of life and for surviving when the tides were really rough.

For those who have suffered depression, stress
and similar psychological problems.
For those who died in their struggle for life and
for those who are still struggling to empower women,
The struggle is longer and harder.

And finally, to all African women who died in their
struggle for life. May the legacy they left behind be upheld.

This book is dedicated to you all.

Table of Contents

Acknowledgements

AkiDWA would like to acknowledge the support and contribution
of the following individuals and organisations.

Ireland Funds
Social Entrepreneur Ireland
FÁS
Amnesty International Ireland
Department of Community, Rural and Gaeltacht Affairs
Combat Poverty Agency
Department of Foreign Affairs – Development Education Cooperation
Dublin Council – Community Development
Dublin Inner City Partnership
Eamonn Henry
Banúlacht
Family Planning Association
Irish Council for Civil Liberties
Catherine McAuley Centre
Integrating Ireland
CREATE
Community Technical Aid
Cáirde
Ronit Lentin
Metro Eireann newspaper
Africa Centre
Irish Refugee Council
NCCRI
Access Ireland
National Women's Council of Ireland
Women's Aid
Mohammed Haji
Sr Joan McManus

INTRODUCTION
Challenges Faced by Women

For centuries women have been spinning invisible threads of love, relationships and communication between different members of the family, and weaving webs of trust and co-operation between different groups in the community. As carers of the world they care for their homes, babies, husbands, the old and elderly, the needs of the family and many other things. They carry this care burden, for ages being denied access to decent, well-paid jobs with career prospects, which could support their life-long economic independence. Women's work in the home is often taken for granted. All over the world women are always discriminated against. In many countries, especially in Africa, women earn less than men, are prevented from owning land and face numerous obstacles to holding positions of authority and many threats of violence. In most cases women are seen as second-class citizens in their own country. It is estimated that there are over 30 million people in the world who are refugees and about 80% of them are women. In most traditional African societies, women work extremely hard and 80% of the food produced on the farm is by them. Their access to economic resources, incomes and employment is poor. It is inherently unfair and unequal that, in many countries, women don't get the same allowances, credits and priorities as men in the employment structure. Men are seen as the breadwinners, women as dependants.

Women migrate to different parts of the world for different reasons and under different circumstances. A large number of them flee their countries for reasons ranging from conflict, natural disasters and repeated human rights abuses. Some say they flee in fear for their lives and for freedom, some in search of food, shelter and better living standards. Others say they migrate for greener pastures, better job opportunities and education. Those who flee in fear for their lives are forced to use any method of escape available to them. These methods include walking, sailing, driving, stowing away on trucks or vans and flying. Very often their journeys are treacherous and some of them end up not surviving.

Ireland has in the last five years experienced a steady and large influx of women from different parts of Africa and different reasons have been given for this change. Most of these women tell tales of slave labour, violence, murder, torture and destitution back home. Living conditions for many African women are inhuman and miserable.

In Africa, millions are displaced within their own countries and though these people are not recognised as refugees in their own countries, they are often just as vulnerable. Repressive leaders and rulers displace their own people. It is far harder to help someone who is displaced within a country than a refugee outside their country because aid and protection gets to internal refugees only when the government allows it. Most wars are actually within and not between countries, especially in Africa, and the gender most hit by these wars is women.

Women experience violence because they are women and often because they do not have the same rights as men. The African Commission of Human and Peoples' Rights in Banjul, Gambia, at one time in a communiqué deplored the prevailing human rights situations of women in nine African countries. The countries named were Algeria, Cameroon, Chad, the Democratic Republic of Congo, Mauritania, Nigeria, Rwanda, Eastern Sierra Leone and Sudan. The commission cited slavery, lack of freedom of expression and association, forced deportations, extra-judicial executions, religious intolerance and political repression. In addition, female genital mutilation (circumcision) was singled out as one of the most widespread violations of the rights of African women in many African countries.

In developing countries nearly 600,000 women die of childbirth every year according to UNICEF. One in four women dies or is seriously disabled from causes related to pregnancy and childbirth. At one time, the country recording the highest death rate was Sierra Leone, with 1,800 deaths for every 100,000 live births. This report by UNICEF said that the situation can only be corrected by addressing the inequalities between men and women, starting with education. The rights of women, including their right to education, their right to dignity and respect, their right to time, to rest, their right to adequate food and health care, are a fundamental part of any permanent solution to the problems faced by women. Today there are many armed conflicts going on around the world forcing women to migrate. Some are attributed to collapsing states, heightened ethnic tensions and violence driven by economic goals. Examples include the diamond extraction in Sierra Leone and battles for oil in Angola and Nigeria. For this reason a lot of women who are affected directly or indirectly but are not able to cope with the situation seek help elsewhere. People who are trapped by war or persecution within their own countries need help as much as, or more than, official refugees and immigrants but the world is slow to appreciate their plight. If more money and effort were put into the development of women worldwide, their economic situation would automatically improve.

Author's Note

It is a privilege to have the great opportunity of being the author of this book. The idea of putting together a book like this was a challenge for me. The experience afforded me the opportunity of getting to the depth of what womanhood really is.

In the course of my sojourn, I met women whose goals and ideals were cut short by the instability created by wars in their countries, giving rise to their sudden movement.

Women fleeing events in their own country and arriving in Ireland, whether accompanied, unaccompanied, alone with children, with or without their partners, face many problems that are specific to their gender. Becoming a refugee or an immigrant in Western society involves a drastic and often painful change in their lives. The loss of the support of the extended family alone is a major blow to them.

For many women who seek refuge in other countries, it is often a personal and emotional struggle. Their stories and circumstances are different but they are all linked by one thing – leaving their countries, homes and often their families for fear of persecution.

A refugee is created when someone is driven by fear to leave his or her home. Refugees are the consequence of a government's failure to protect human rights, depriving them of a decent and dignified life.

Women should be seen as the torch of the world. They have special privileges, special attributes, and are gifted with the intuition to be able to foresee a lot of things.

Every woman I approached was eager to enquire what title AkiDwA intended to give the book. I was bombarded with so many questions whenever I asked a woman for inclusion of 'Her story' in this book. For many of them, there was uncertainty and a feeling of their private life being encroached upon. I was patient. My explanation was for them to share their stories so the world could know their plight. For others, they were eager to inform the world.

However, those whose stories have appeared in this book are courageous and their stories deserve to be heard. I was extremely touched when these stories were related to me. I conducted the interviews in a variety of places to suit each person's request. Some preferred their homes, a few their workplace and others cafés or bars.

From Cameroon to Nigeria, South Africa, Rwanda, Zimbabwe and many other African countries, come these touching true-life experiences and struggles of African women.

The stories in this book, I hope, make a good read, providing insight into the true-life experiences of some African women before they left their countries. The aim of the book is to educate, inform and enlighten the society more about Africa and Africans. My aim has been to write in a way that is accessible to a wide readership.

These are true-life stories. The names are real except for those who requested to remain anonymous. Unbelievable as they may sound, these are true-life evidences that there is chaos and unrest in Africa. The proven facts and tales are there to tell. Inter-state wars may be visible but internal conflicts are gradually wiping out generations, often invisibly. Disasters are not peculiar to any particular race. They can happen in any country and to anyone. No one knows when they might be forced to flee or seek shelter and protection in a place that is not their own. Seeking help, shelter and escape from ordeal is not a taboo and victims should not be treated as outcasts.

This is the time to act. Let us make a positive impact on the lives of people. Let us not continue to fold our arms and watch generations waste. Let us not allow our reasoning to be clouded by sentiments.

Understanding and appreciating the values of women, given their sad experiences and touched by the various stories of the lives of the African women that I have met, I am glad that I took up this project.

I wish to thank those who courageously agreed to be interviewed for this book. Without them, this book would never have come into being. I am touched by their struggle to make something meaningful out of life. I thank them sincerely for sharing their stories and their visions, which hopefully will enlighten, inform, challenge and inspire people.

As a freelance journalist I have had the privilege of working with seasoned professionals who in one way or another have influenced my life positively. This book has been made possible by the support, encouragement and advice of such people and also by my family, friends, acquaintances and contacts.

My appreciation goes to the AkiDwA organisation with special thanks to Salome Mbugua, founder of the organisation, for trusting and believing in my abilities, Roddy Doyle for encouraging me and supporting my efforts, Alphonso Oladepo Ogunwusi for his technical and moral support and for providing me with vital materials to make this project a success. I am also thankful to Mojisola Oduola-Falola for her effort, encouragement and sleepless nights at the time I started this book. And finally to Tina Tinuke-Jinad, Chinedu Onyejelem, Anthony Afolo and Mercy Ebun Peters for their contributions and invaluable support

To everyone who has contributed to this book, I am extremely grateful, and I say a big thank you to you all.

Pamela Toyin Akinjobi

AkiDwA
(African Women's Network)

In 2001 a number of African women in Ireland saw the necessity to come together to encourage community initiatives amongst immigrants, refugees and asylum seekers as well as to make positive impacts in the society they have chosen as their home. It was also important to provide African women with support and a platform to speak for themselves, to assist them in taking a new step of hope and to facilitate them to integrate better into Irish society. Such was the initiative of Salome Mbugua, a Kenyan woman, who founded AkiDwA.

With a burning urge to create a forum where the problems, expectations and desires of African women could be expressed and examined, Salome founded AkiDwA as a culturally appropriate medium to provide a social network for African women in Ireland and to respond to their existing and changing needs. AkiDwA was established in August 2001 by seven African women living in Ireland, natives of Zimbabwe, Kenya, Nigeria, Tanzania, Zambia, Rwanda and Congo.

Akina Dada wa Africa (AkiDwA), the Swahili version of African sisterhood, serves as a representative body for all African women living in Ireland, irrespective of their national/ethnic background, traditional religious beliefs, socio-economic or legal status.

AkiDwA's mission is to promote equality for African women living in Ireland so as to encourage social justice.

Fundamental to its work is the belief that women's rights are human rights. AkiDwA recognise that African women face particular barriers to their empowerment. As a result the following human rights charter underpins its work:-
- A right to be free from Racism, Discrimination and Stereotyping
- A right to live Free of Poverty
- A right to be Valued for the full diversity of their situation & conditions
- A right to be respected as Equals in Irish Society,
- A right to live Free from Abuse Personally, Socially and Politically
- A right to live Free from Violence within Relationships
- A right to Determine Our Own Needs and the Responses to these needs

- A right to an Equal Voice in all areas of our lives
- A right to an Education
- A right to Work
- A right to be Healthy
- A right to be Confident and Happy.

The long-term aim of the organisation is to establish a multi-purpose resource centre so as to address and meet the needs of migrant women fully.

In their struggle to continue to empower women, AkiDwA planned three projects in 2002. These projects were Developing African Women's Network, Women, Race and Cultural Diversity and Herstory. The purpose of the first two projects was to develop a strong African women's network that will highlight issues affecting black and ethnic minority women around the country and which will link the national bodies to influence policy. It was also meant to facilitate people to understand how racism and other forms of discrimination develop, to highlight the consequences of institutional racism going unchallenged, to allow people to examine changes in the lives of women as a result of the global women's movement as well as to ensure that diversity of traditions, religion and countries are valued.

The aim of Herstory is:

- To facilitate some of the most vulnerable African women living in Ireland to share their migration stories, past traumas and struggles
- To examine their future options by assisting and supporting them to attain their goals
- To enable them deal with past trauma
- The ten chapters of this book provide insights into the true-life experiences of some African women before they left their countries. The book seeks to educate, inform and enlighten the society more about Africa and Africans as well as to challenge false impressions about asylum-seekers and immigrants.

Currently AkiDwA's work is dictated by its five-year strategic plan. The following projects commenced last year:

"Violence against Women": AkiDwA's work on violence initially started in 2003, though last year three awareness-raising seminars were held in three counties, reaching 75 migrant women. AkiDwA is also a member of the advisory committee with Amnesty International Ireland in their international campaign on violence against women. AkiDwA hopes to carry out research on this issue. The organisation continues to collaborate and work with Women's Aid and the Immigrant Council of Ireland.

"Female Genital Mutilation": AkiDwA is a leading member of the coalition against FGM. With the other groups that are involved, AkiDwA continues to raise awareness and provide education on the issue as well advocate for legislation that would ban FGM being practised in Ireland. AkiDwA also believes that the Irish government should consider FGM as a gender-specific crime that should be considered in the asylum process. AkiDwA has recently conducted three focus group discussions and work on this issue is ongoing.

"Health needs of African women": mental health, reproductive health and awareness raising on check-ups for breast and cervical cancer are some of our major areas of focus in health.

Gender and Racism": racism has been and continues to be a huge problem in Ireland. AkiDwA has done significant work on this issue, which includes offering training to women who have in turn visited schools and other institutions to challenge racism. It has become apparent that racism affects women differently from men. There is no doubt that the interface of racism for black and ethnic-minority women is related to their gender – as women, mothers, carers, black – and to their religion and dress code.

These four projects were identified by women themselves through needs assessment carried out in 2003. AkiDwA's work is therefore to facilitate a platform where women can gain awareness, share their experiences and articulate ways they can tackle some of the problems that they encounter. In addition, AkiDwA, with its allies, is committed to lobby for change at the national level.

AkiDwA will develop submission papers from the four projects by 2007.

Prologue

Though the weather that particular day was steaming hot, Emma's body shook with cold in her prison room. She was pregnant from a brutal rape by a policeman and, even though she was just in her third month, she felt all the signs of labour. She struggled for an old cracked chair by her bed but her knees gave way and she slumped. She was so weak she could hardly hear her own scream for help.

Violet went from house to house begging people to buy the second-hand clothes she sold. Her week-old baby needed food and clothes. At the end of each day, she retired to a dilapidated building she shared with tramps and destitutes.

Lydia heard a loud thud. She removed her shoes and tiptoed to the window from where the sound came. Her body froze with shock at what she saw. Her friend's hands were tied to the back of the chair on which she sat. She had been stripped naked and there were whip marks all over her body.

Carefully shielded behind a pole, Nina watched Onome go through the gruesome ordeal of female circumcision. An ear-splitting scream seized the air as the grip of five hefty men bit hard into Onome's skin, forcefully pinning her body to the ground. Beads of sweat laced her forehead and her body shook with agonising, excruciating pains.

You could feel the presence of poverty staring you in the face. The air in the neighbourhood was foul with urine, harsh and graceless. Though the house looked simple and neat, everything else spelt poverty. The extent of this poverty fired Chileshe's determination to equip herself and her siblings with a good education, the most potent weapon against poverty.

The disaster on the television was unbelievable. Burnt wood, chips of metal, broken glass as well as burnt bodies filled the streets. The sight was terrifying, gory and nauseating. The country was at stake. By the time the news was over, Iye Jillo's eyes were swollen shut with tears. Her boss and mentor of many years had been killed.

The journey to the camp lasted three gruesome hours. Women cried as they were dragged out of the van. Dead bodies were also dragged out of the van. Like slaves in the nineteenth century, they followed the orders of their captors as they were marched into different rooms in the bungalow. Mary sat down on the floor in a corner and watched as other frightened faces joined her.

Students took to the street in a massive peaceful demonstration. As they protested openly, policemen shot at them in cold blood. There was chaos as Mora and many others ran for their lives. Suddenly, she heard a bang, followed by another, and then, another. She felt a weight pull her down. She looked frantically around. Ella, her friend, lay in a pool of her own blood. She had been hit.

A loud bang echoed in the distance, waking the whole neighbourhood. Joyce got up startled. The clock beside her bed confirmed her fears. It was 3 a.m. Someone outside the house screamed for help as hurried footsteps passed outside her door. Then she heard another bang. A few seconds later the air was filled with smoke and in the twinkle of an eye the house was engulfed in fire.

The bulldozer moved into action raising its dreadful jaw. Moji wailed as her shop was being demolished. It was her only source of income, her last hope and all she depended on. It was unbelievable.

Cameroon at a Glance

History: Little was known about Cameroon before 1472 when the Portuguese arrived shouting 'Camarões, Camarões!' in amazement at the many giant shrimp – hence the country's name. For the next 400 years, southern Cameroon's history, like that of the rest of West Africa's Atlantic seaboard, revolved around the slave trade. Northern Cameroon, by contrast, was a battleground for various empires, notably the Kanem-Bornu in Chad. When the Germans arrived in the late 19th century, 'feudal' northern Cameroon was under the control of the Fulani empire in Sokoto (Nigeria). Shaped a bit like a boat, Cameroon is bordered by Nigeria to the north and west, Chad and the Central African Republic to the east, Congo, Gabon and Equatorial Guinea to the south and the Atlantic Ocean to the west. Despite an invitation from a Douala chief to set up a protectorate over the area in the 1850s, Great Britain dallied for decades and finally lost to the Germans in 1884, who beat them to an agreement by five days. The Germans were active colonisers, building schools, railways and plantations, but their rule was harsh. At one plantation a fifth of the labourers died in a single year from overwork. After World War I Cameroon received new overlords from the League of Nations, which gave the French a mandate over 80% of the territory and the British control of two separate areas, one in the south-western highlands (southern Cameroons) and the other in the north (northern Cameroons, now part of Nigeria). As a result, a single nation was divided into three parts governed by two colonial powers – hardly a situation conducive to later unification. Within a few years the British sold their Cameroons holdings back to the Germans, who didn't last much longer. The outbreak of World War II saw them repatriated and stripped of their land by the Allies. By contrast, the French improved the railways (with forced labour, forbidden by their mandate), developed cocoa and palm oil plantations and exported timber, increasing the value of trade fivefold in its portion of the country between the world wars. After World War II, new political parties formed in French Cameroon pressed for independence. A northern-based party, the 'Union Camerounaise', gained control of the national assembly, aggravating the resentment of southerners. Following independence in 1960, the resentment blossomed into a full-scale rebellion that took five battalions of French troops and a squadron of fighter planes eight months to put down. Thousands were ruthlessly killed and a state of emergency that lasted two decades was declared. The 'Union Camerounaise' held onto power and its leader, a northerner and an ardent Muslim, became president. The former French Cameroon and part of British Cameroon merged in 1961 to form the present country.

Cameroon has generally enjoyed stability, which has permitted the development of agriculture, roads and railways, as well as a petroleum industry. Despite movement toward democratic reform, political power remained firmly in the hands of an ethnic oligarchy. In 1961, northern Cameroons voted to become part of Nigeria. The south opted for federation with French Cameroon, forming a single republic 11 years later. The President's positive contribution was to invest wisely in agriculture, education, health care and roads, while resisting the temptation to borrow heavily and build expensive show projects. As a result, school enrolment reached 70% and farms produced enough food to keep the country self-sufficient and to export a wide range of commodities. At the height of his power and success, the President unexpectedly announced his resignation in 1982. His handpicked successor, a prime minister who was a southerner and a Christian, immediately set about removing the previous president's northern cronies, known as the 'barons'. By 1984, the barons staged a coup that almost succeeded but the new president quickly regained control and was re-elected unopposed in 1988. In 1990, furious with his inept handling of the economy, Cameroonians began openly accusing the government of corruption and formed a new party, the Social Democratic Front (SDF). The government's murderous attempt to wipe out the new threat backfired, and in less than a year there were 30 political parties and nearly a dozen independent newspapers. Because of the government's refusal to call a constitutional convention in 1991, strikes brought the country to a standstill. Eventually the first multi-party elections were called in over 30 years. Various opposition parties took 52% of the vote. Later that year, the President won again when he was re-elected as president, defeating scattered and unprepared opposition. His victory prompted accusations of electoral fraud from international observers and set off widespread rioting in western

Cameroon. The government devalued the CFA franc in 1994, raising exports and sending the public-sector salaries plunging to 70%. Soon after the National Assembly (dominated by the Union Camerounaise) extended the presidential term from five years to seven, the President won in 1997 for the third time, this time unopposed but with less than a third of voters bothering to turn out.

Economy: Because of its oil resources and favourable agricultural conditions, Cameroon has one of the best-endowed primary commodity economies in sub-Saharan Africa. Still, it faces many serious problems like top-heavy civil service and a generally unfavourable climate for business enterprise similar to that facing other underdeveloped countries.

Since 1990, the government has embarked on various IMF and World Bank programmes designed to spur business investment, increase efficiency in agriculture, improve trade and recapitalise the nation's banks. In June 2000, the government completed an IMF-sponsored three-year structural adjustment program; however, the IMF is pressing for more reforms, including increased budget transparency and privatisation. International oil and cocoa prices have considerable impact on the economy, including petroleum production and refining, food processing, light consumer goods, textiles, lumber, coffee, cocoa, cotton, rubber, bananas, oilseed, grains, root starches, livestock and timber.

Population: The population of Cameroon is over 16 million with 730,000 in its capital city Yaoundé. The Highlanders make 31%, Equatorial Bantus 19%, Kirdis 11%, Fulanis 10%, North-western Bantus 8%, Eastern Nigritics 7%, other Africans 13% and non-Africans less than 1%.

Languages: There are 24 major African language groups in Cameroon. Both French and English are official languages, though French is more widely spoken, especially in large modern cities such as Yaoundé and Douala. About 10% of the country relies primarily on 'pidgin' or 'broken' English – mainly in the western provinces near Nigeria. Among the many African languages spoken in Cameroon, the five major ones are Bamiléké, Ewondo, Bamoun, Fulfulde and Arabic.

Culture: With sweltering rainforests and strutting sultans, wildlife parks and grilled chicken, Cameroon is one of Africa's most naturally and culturally diverse countries. Though the south is more European, until the 20th century the north was part of quasi-feudal Muslim Fulani kingdoms centred in Nigeria. Traditions and cultures practised in the French-speaking part, the English-speaking part and the adopted traditions from the part close to Nigeria make Cameroon an interesting, multicultural society. Up till now, its traditions and resistance to outside influence remains strong.

Ethnic groups: In addition to its French and British colonial past, there are over 130 ethnic groups in the country speaking dozens of languages. Cameroon's split English/French personality is further complicated by its bewildering array of African ethnic groups and languages. Of over 130 ethnic groups, however, there are 5 major ones. Bamiléké and Bamoun in the West, Fulani and Kirdi in the North, and Ewondo around Yaoundé. The Bamiléké are the most populous group in the western highlands and one of the largest communities in Douala, where they have taken control of much of Cameroon's economy. In their rural homeland, there are some 80-odd political units ruled by strongly independent chefferies (chiefs).

Within each unit there are numerous secret societies responsible for the preservation of rituals. By contrast, the Bamoun are governed by a single leader called the sultan. Most northerners, however, are neither Fulani nor Muslim but Kirdi (the Fulani word for pagan). The Kirdi are comprised of tribes driven by the Fulani into the inhospitable and isolated rocky areas near the Nigerian border.

Religion: In Cameroon there are Christians, Muslims and those that fall under the indigenous beliefs. Islam and Christianity compete for souls, as do an array of traditional animist beliefs.

Food: Cameroon has some of the best food in Central Africa. Manioc leaves are one of the main ingredients, usually appearing on menus as feuille. Sauces are usually accompanied by rice (riz), or a thick mashed potato-like substance that comes in three main forms: couscous, pâe or fufu. Any of these can be made from rice, corn, manioc, plantains or bananas. Street food is typically excellent, consisting mainly of grilled spiced brochettes stuffed into a bread roll with salad and dressing. The lively African quarters of Messa, Mokolo and Briqueterie, a few kilometres northwest of downtown Yaoundé, are where you'll find many of the city's unlicensed chicken houses, serving the best grilled chicken.

Tourist attractions: The best prospects for hiking in Cameroon are the northern area between the towns of Rumsiki and Mora and the eastern area around Bamenda. Mt Cameroon offers excellent rock climbing. There's also good climbing in Mindif, a park south of the northern town of Maroua, where few have succeeded in mastering a huge rock known as 'le Dent de Mindif'.

Yaoundé: Once a sleepy colonial capital, Yaoundé, which has particularly good grilled chicken and fish, is now a bustling urban centre of meandering streets and undulating hills, offering an unusually cool climate and excellent museums. 'Ave Kennedy' is the main commercial corridor at its northern end and in the centre is Artisinal, a giant tent filled with local artisans and their handicrafts. A few kilometres north of the city centre is the Benedictine monastery's Musée d'Art Cameroonais, a highlight of any visit to the capital. Despite its small size, it has one of the best collections of Cameroonian art in the world, including masks, bowls and Bamoun bronze pipes. Even the monastery's chapel is decorated with a beautiful array of local textiles and crafts. The monastery is near the foot of Mt Fébé and is accessible by bus or taxi from downtown.

A few kilometres west of downtown is the Quartier Melen, home to the Musée d'Art Nègre. The museum's collection includes Bamoun pipes from north-west Cameroon, Baoulé textiles from Côte d'Ivoire and Congolese-Zaïrian masks, as well as pieces from Algeria and Ethiopia. Melen is also home to the 'Paroisse de N'Djong Melen', a church with an interesting open-air Sunday mass. For over two hours, a priest recites the mass in Ewondo to the accompaniment of African drumming, dancing and singing.

Outside of the swelling and modernised cities of Yaoundé, the capital, and Douala, the largest city and industrial centre, rainforests stretch north from the Atlantic Ocean, giving way to savannah and semi-desert in the north. Elephants and bongos congregate by the hundreds in some of Africa's best wildlife parks, and beachcombers laze on long, isolated beaches.

Douala: Douala does have a couple of interesting sights of its own. It is a good base for exploring much more interesting places. Kribi, Limbe and Mt Cameroon are all within a few hours' journey. A kilometre to the south-west is the 'Musée de Douala' (Douala Museum) located in the hôtel de ville in the town hall. Filled with mostly mediocre Bamoun and Bamiléké pieces, the museum is free and by studying its exhibits tourists will be better able to judge the craftwork for sale on the streets. The best place for artefacts is the 'Artisianal Camerounais', an open-air crafts market located about halfway between the Akwa Palace and the town hall.

Foumban: Though slightly touristy, Foumban is one of Cameroon's major attractions and an important centre of traditional African art. Its jewel is the 'Palais Royal' (Royal Palace) the seat of power of the Bamoun people. The palace, which was completed in 1917, resembles a medieval chateau. It houses the Sultan's Museum, which contains a multitude of royal gowns, arms, musical instruments, statues, jewellery, masks and colourful bead-covered thrones carved in the shapes of the men who sat on them. A few hundred metres south of the palace is the 'Musée des Arts' (Arts Museum). Its extensive collection has exhibits on Bamoun history and art, including cooking implements, musical instruments, pipes, statues, masks, gongs and an ornately carved xylophone. The road that connects the two museums is home to sculptors, basket makers, weavers, embroiderers and one of the best places in Central Africa to buy woodcarvings.

Buea & Mt Cameroon (The Cameroon mountain in Buea): Buea offers a refreshingly cool climate and an invigorating 10,000-foot climb up Mt Cameroon. The town's main sight is the Mountain Hotel, which has a rustic English charm.

Parc National du Waza (The National Park in Waza): Waza has some of central Africa's best wildlife, though its scrubby, flat terrain isn't particularly scenic. The major attraction is the hundreds of pachyderms that congregate at 'Mare aux Eléphants', the main watering hole. The park's many species of bird life include hornbills, ostriches, crested cranes, herons and storks. The best time of year to see animals is from March to May, which is also the hottest season.

CHAPTER ONE

Emma
Cameroon

It was the 20th of May, the National Day in Cameroon. It was a travel free day for everyone in the country. The National Day in Cameroon is a day set aside for all the citizens of the country to express their freedom of speech, freedom to rejoice and freedom to do whatever pleases them as long as it is in line with the law of the country. The activities of the day usually included a marching parade by students. Sometimes peaceful demonstrations were also included, if there was a need for them.

For Emma, that day began, like any other day, in prison. She had been through so much that she had lost hope of ever getting out of the place alive. A police officer, who had been a great help to her in the past, had promised he was going to help her get her freedom whenever an opportunity presented itself. But, day after day, the little hope Emma had, had faded as things became more difficult for her. She knew he was working alone against a brutal force. She knew it was impossible for just one man to get her away from the jaws of several others who didn't care if she lived or died.

His own life was also at risk because of the special care he showed towards her. Several times in the past, he had sneaked in food for her when she was left to starve as a form of punishment. He had been labelled bad because of her and often he had faced threats from his superiors. He had been particularly kind to her because he was aware of what had led to her arrest and he knew she was being treated unjustly. He was also bitter about what had happened the day she was brutally raped in prison. Since then he had vowed to do anything and everything possible to get her out of the prison, even if it would cost him his job. He knew it was just a matter of time. He was prepared to wait until he was sure he could carry out his plans. For weeks he tried to map out a strategy around an idea that kept nagging him and, each time, he came to a conclusion. Everything revolved around the National Day. It was the best, and probably the only, opportunity he would ever have to save Emma. Apart from the fact that he had control over the prison that day, it was a perfect day for anyone to get away with anything without being noticed. Unknown to Emma, he began to make plans for her to escape.

Emma was curled up in a corner when the policeman approached her prison door. She had not been feeling well for days and her pregnancy had made her condition worse. She got up and managed a smile. She stared at the policeman with shock and watched as he opened the prison door, where she had been locked in isolation for four months. It was like a dream. It was unbelievable. Her knees went weak. She stared at him in shock. He shook her back to life and handed her a school uniform. He had figured that the best way for her to sneak out was dressed as one of the students doing the Marching Parade that day. Hurriedly, with shaking hands, Emma changed into the uniform. When she was dressed the policeman gave her some money and, helping her out of the building, he urged her to run as fast as she could along a footpath located at the back of the police station. There was no time. His colleagues could show up any minute. Gratitude and tears welled up in Emma as she made her way out of the place she regarded as hell. She had experienced torture, rape and violence in the four months she had spent in prison. Her escape that morning had been miraculous and with every breath that came out of her came prayers for the man who had set her free. It had been so sudden and so unexpected that she thought she was going to wake up realising that it was all a dream. The last thing she had expected was freedom.

The weather that particular morning was hot and humid. From fear and heat, Emma dripped with sweat. She wiped her forehead as she ran along the footpath. For the first five minutes, she didn't look back. She came to a major road. Out in the open, she slowed her pace to catch her breath, clutching a tattered carrier bag containing all she had. She made her way through a dark alley towards the parade square. She was relieved. It was the safest way to go. She was weak and needed somewhere to rest her feet until she could think of what to do next. She thought of her pregnancy and how she was going to cope for the remaining months. The rape she had experienced in prison had resulted in pregnancy but that was the least of her worries. All she wanted was to be free again, to find help.

Emma was frail and emaciated, and the long walk made her tired.

She couldn't wait to be united once again with her mother and brothers, and the thought urged her to continue. She dragged her feet and, as she made her way through the dark alley, she heard a low whistle behind her. Suddenly she froze. She was scared of looking back. A few more steps and she would be out of the alley, into the open street. Her heart raced and she quickened her footsteps. As she did this, the footsteps behind her seemed to quicken, and this made her panic.

She was sure that whoever was behind her was after her. She was sure that news had leaked that she had escaped, and the search for her was on. She was tempted to run but resisted, as it might turn into a disaster. She knew she couldn't run, no matter how hard she tried. She hurried on, determined to get to the open street.

Then something happened. Something dropped from her hand. It was the money the policeman had given her. She almost screamed. It was all she had and she couldn't afford to lose it. She picked it up as quickly as she could, before the person behind her caught up with her. As she picked up the money, a male hand gripped her wrist.

Emma froze. Her body shook. Her heart raced.

'Hello, Emma.'

A man pulled her up.

Emma let out an ear-splitting scream as the man tried to cover her mouth. Struggling to free her hand, she looked up. It was her cousin. A mixture of relief and anxiety welled up in her. She broke into tears. He had been to the police station, and the officer who had helped her had explained the event of that day to him. Still trying to catch her breath from the shock, she walked to a nearby kerb and sat down. Her legs shook and she felt as if she was going to pass out. For several minutes she kept mute, holding her hands against her chest. When she was fully recovered, her cousin walked her to the parade square where thousands of people watched as students entertained them. Emma and her cousin sat down, away from the crowd. The event was colourful but Emma hardly noticed what was going on. The memories of the event that had led to her being locked up for four months kept nagging at her mind.

Emma's father was a polygamist with five wives and her mother, who had seven children, was the last of the five. Her father had thirty-six children in all, and they all lived together in a big hut in Baliaumbat

Village where her father farmed. Most of his children worked on his cocoa and coffee farm daily because he couldn't afford to send them all to school. After working on her father's farm Emma would also help her mother on her groundnut and corn maize farm. At night, eight of them slept in one bed because they had just a few beds to share between them all. The five wives were friendly with each other and they treated all the children as theirs. Every day the wives took it in turn to cook enough food to feed as many children as they could. The food would be served in a very big bowl so all the children could eat together. The children would happily gather around the big bowl and eat with their hands. The faster they were, the more they ate. Emma's mother saved each day and when Emma was eight years old her mother sent her to school. She was determined to send all of her own children to school, no matter how late. Every morning, Emma would wake up early to help her mother on the farm. After that, she fetched water for her and then went to school.

Emma found it very difficult mixing with the other pupils. She was very tall for her age and the oldest in her class. She was always ashamed in school and her interest in her studies began to diminish.

On one particular day, Emma forgot to fetch water for her mother. Her mother realised this just when Emma was leaving for school, and even though Emma was dressed up and almost late, her mother insisted Emma had to fetch the water. Dragging a bucket behind her, Emma went to the stream. In her hurry back home, she slipped and fell in mud, messing up her school uniform. Her mother beat her, saying she'd done it deliberately because she didn't want to go to school.

After a year in school, a special request was made by Emma's mother for her daughter to be put in a class of her age group. Emma was made to skip the next two classes and was promoted to the third class. But, rather than improving her situation, she found it hard to learn in the class and this affected her studies a great deal. She hardly understood what was being taught and her academic performance deteriorated. At the end of it all, she barely scraped through with a pass. But rather than lose hope, Emma was determined to go on to secondary school. Emma attended school more regularly. She was determined to excel. Her determination helped her through and she began to learn fast. Her academic performance improved drastically.

She made top grades in no time and soon became one of the best in her class. Her father doted on her and promised to support her as best as he could.

One day in her second year in secondary school, at the age of fifteen, Emma's father sent for her at school. He ordered her to leave school immediately and see him at home. Emma was alarmed. She ran home. As she approached her father's hut she saw a group of people and her mother engrossed in a serious discussion. She knew something was amiss. She sat outside, wondering what could be happening. After the discussion, her father summoned her in and introduced her to the gathering. He told her he was giving her away in marriage to the oldest man in the group. He was a chief in the village and known to have 28 wives. The chief was 45 years old. Emma's father explained to her that he had chosen her because she was her mother's first daughter and her mother was his last wife. Emma and her mother protested but he gave them no option to challenge anything he said: his decision was final.

The chief left with a grin on his face. Emma cried to her mother who promised to find a solution to the problem.

While thinking of what to do, Emma and her mother played along with her father until one of her brothers came to her rescue. He had been living and working in Yaoundé, the capital city of Cameroon, for years. He had come to the village on a visit. He was amused by what he heard and he stressed to his mother that it would be unwise to let Emma continue going to school in the village. He was sure if she did, she would be kidnapped and taken to the palace of the chief. He suggested that, since it was no longer safe for Emma to remain in the village, the best thing was for him to take her away with him to Yaoundé. Secret plans were made and Emma left with him. Her father was shocked and ashamed when he discovered. He lost his prestige and pride in the village. He was mocked because his daughter had run away from him. He was labelled a greedy man. In anger, he disowned Emma and her brother, insisting her brother should take on the role of a father to her and also be responsible for paying her bride price when she was ready to marry. From then on, Emma's responsibilities became her brother's. She lived with him and took care of his children. Emma stayed at home awaiting a new life.

After three years she was back in school again and, this time, she was not only too old to be in her class but had grown very big and tall. She became really ashamed of going to school and sitting in the same class with students who were much younger than her. This affected her so much that all she had learnt in school in the past was not reflected in her life. She faced the situation and passed out of secondary school. In the end, she was admitted into a typing school. Two years after, she graduated and got her first job in an electronics shop as a typist. Even though her father had disowned her, Emma made it her duty to send him her first salary when she learnt he had lost all his money to politics. (It is customary in many countries in Africa for children to share their first salary with their family. The head of the family or the parents of the child would pray on the money before sharing it among members of the family as a sign of blessing. This signified that progress would follow the child at work and that the child would make a hundred fold of that first salary). The good gesture touched Emma's father's heart. In appreciation, he wrote her a moving thank-you letter, saying the money came as a surprise because he thought she was dead. Emma worked in the electronics shop for three years, until 1993, when she went back to the village and sold all she had to support her father in his political campaign.

During the preparation for the presidential election in Cameroon, Emma's father had been appointed by his party, the SDF, to run a special campaign in Baliaumbat village where he lived, because of his popularity and his involvement in politics. Emma's father loved politics and his life was devoted to it. He summoned his children, friends and associates to rally round and assist him in any way they could. His children helped him with the campaign and Emma took time off from work in the city and went to the village to join the others. When the campaign began, Emma's father started to shuttle between his village, Baliaumbat, and Yaoundé to strengthen his contacts. With money and power, he got supporters and more followers for his party. He began to gain ground. As he made progress, he made enemies in the opposing party. Rumours went around that he was trying to destroy or buy-off key figures in the opposing party. His opponents began to see him as a threat, especially when they realised many of their supporters had left their party for his. They hatched a plan. It was to teach him a lesson that would shake his followers.

On one of his trips to Yaounde, Emma's father was captured. He was taken into hiding where he was brutally tortured and killed. Secretly, his corpse was taken to his house and hidden. For years, Emma's father had banned his children and wives from entering a room he regarded as sacred in the house. No one knew what went on inside this room, and no one dared to ask him. In the days after he was killed, no one suspected anything. His wives and children assumed he was away in the city, busy with the plans for the election. Suspicions arose when, a few weeks later, his wives and children noticed flies coming out from under the door of the sacred room. The alarm was raised and the door was broken down. In the room was the decomposed corpse of Emma's father. The sight was terrible. No one knew when and how he got there or who put him there. His children were horrified. His wives were devastated. The whole village mourned him for weeks. It was a terrible blow for, not just his family, but also his political supporters.

After her father's funeral, Emma lost her job because she had stayed too long in the village. After searching for a few months, she got a job as a typist with the Cameroon Times. This was a dream come true for Emma. The prospects were good and the pay was not too bad. She was happy. The job not only gave her good experience; it also gave her the opportunity of contributing articles to the newspaper. In less than a year, Emma had made considerable progress. Her skills had improved.

The shock of the discovery of their father's body made his children vow to avenge his death. In a bid to do this, they faced a determination by the government to crush them. Not caring what happened, the children went on with their plans. Two of Emma's brothers were arrested and locked up: they are still missing.

Emma decided to publish the story, believing that the culprits would be apprehended and her brothers would be released. She published an article on how their father was murdered by agents working for the government. After the publication she began to get threatening phone calls at work. She paid no serious attention to them because she was confident she was safe and would be protected by her employers. She approached her editor and reported the threats. He promised to help in any way he could. But when she was arrested and locked up, a few days after the article was published, no one, not even her boss, could do anything. They were up against power and money, the root of the evil behind the force that ruled the country.

The first month in prison, no one in her family knew Emma's whereabouts. No one knew what had happened to her until the policeman who eventually helped her escape went in search of her family and informed them of where she was.

In prison, Emma suffered from depression. She was roughly handled and told that her life would be reduced to nothing and finally snuffed out if she tried to play smart. Emma was frustrated. She became stubborn and unruly. She misbehaved and constantly rained abuse on the prison officials. In anger, the police commissioner threatened her and promised to make her life more unbearable. A few weeks later, Emma was blindfolded with a scarf and dragged out of her prison cell by four policemen into a room in a building used by the police for special interrogations. She was tied to a table. Three of the men then disappeared, leaving her with one man. While she was still blindfolded, the man tore open her dress. Emma screamed and cried for help as he brutally raped her, but no one came to her rescue. She bled afterwards and, for days, she couldn't sit with her legs together. Some police officers made fun of her and told her that the police commissioner had specifically given instructions for her to be raped. No one paid her any attention or offered any form of help. She was made a laughing stock. She was constantly tortured and hardly fed. Her health deteriorated and, some weeks after the rape, she discovered she was pregnant. She cried her eyes out but, rather than attracting sympathy, she experienced more hostility. There was no one to turn to, no one to complain to and nowhere to go. She was scared that if she tried anything silly, she would pay with her life.

Slowly she began to succumb to the orders that were dished out to her. Like a chameleon, she decided to change her colour to suit her environment, until she could find a way out. And finally that day had come.

Emma heaved a sigh. The parade was still going on. She needed to rest. Her cousin hid her in a house in Douala. Her pregnancy was a constant reminder of the past. She thought of aborting it but dismissed the idea when she couldn't get any money. Even though she hated the pregnancy, she took a decision to have the baby. She couldn't go

29

through the stress of abortion. She was sure her health was not good enough to go through another ordeal.

Week after week, Emma became more depressed. She withdrew, hardly conversing with anyone. Often she forgot who she was. She lost her values and almost lost her senses. She was scared of going out in case she was spotted or recognised and rearrested again and, every time the doorbell rang, she sprang up, startled. A few times, when she saw the glimpse of the uniform of a policeman through the window, she shivered and screamed in agony. She believed all the policemen in the street were after her life.

For months she stayed at home, dreading the thought of being caught and sent back to prison. Her flatmate, Blessing, became worried and arranged for the pastor of her church to visit Emma at home, to pray for her.

Emma's health did not improve and, in the seventh month of her pregnancy, she had a miscarriage. She bled so much that she thought she was going to die. Even with the memories of her trauma, she felt bad after losing a life that had become a part of her.

A few months later Blessing's boyfriend, Joshua, arranged with his business partner to take Emma to Ivory Coast. Joshua traded in aluminium products, which often took him to different parts of Africa. His business partners in Ivory Coast were Cameroonians. He was sure the change would make a difference in Emma's life. It was a welcome relief for Emma. She was eager to start a new life. Soon she put the loss of her pregnancy behind her. Her life began to take a new shape. She started to regain her senses and confidence started to build up in her again. Her trip to Ivory Coast was a different experience for her and, within a few months, she was settled. Joshua's friends set her up in trading in clothes. She got accustomed to the system and worked her way to the top. Slowly but steadily, she climbed the ladder of success. In the course of her work she met Kingsley, another trader. He showed an interest in Emma and they began to date. Soon Kingsley proposed to her. Slowly, Emma began to put the pieces of her life together again. Emma's focus became the future. She made it her duty every week to offer special prayers in church. She constantly prayed for her future and for Kingsley not to end up a polygamist like her father, whose image often flashed through her mind.

Putting her past totally behind her, Emma began to plan her wedding with Kingsley. It was a double blessing for her when she discovered she was pregnant. All the preparations were in place and invitations were sent out. The wedding date was fixed for after the birth of the baby. Kingsley was supportive and he stood by her throughout the pregnancy. One day Emma started to feel labour pains and was taken to a hospital. The day after she was admitted, Kingsley came into the hospital looking sad and jittery. He informed Emma that he needed to travel urgently to Cameroon to see his mother who was ill and dying. Fear gripped Emma but Kingsley patted her stomach and reassured her that he would be back as soon as he could. Before he left for Cameroon, he left enough money with one of his friends to take care of Emma.

A few days later, Emma's baby arrived. It was a girl. One of her friends brought a wedding invitation to the hospital with them. Emma read it, unaware of its contents. The invitation indicated Kingsley was getting married that weekend to another woman in Cameroon. Emma realised that he had deceived her and lied to her. She almost went mad. She shook with rage. She was in shock for a week, hardly eating anything and talking to no one. She had to be constantly reminded by people around her that she had a beautiful baby who needed her.

Two weeks later, Kingsley returned. He lied, saying he had had to spend more time than expected in Cameroon because his mother's situation had become worse. He got a shock when Emma brought out his wedding invitation. He walked out of Emma's life and never returned to her. Emma almost died. She became ill with a blood clot in her brain. She suffered badly from depression and had to be placed under special care. She did not recuperate for several months.

Single-handedly, Emma slaved and brought up her child, Joy, alone. Her only happiness was watching Joy grow. She was determined to give her the best of everything in life and a better education than she had had as a child.

Emma worked hard and after a few years she established her own business. Once again, Emma's life changed as she became fully established in Ivory Coast. She watched as Joy blossomed into a lovely little girl. Life became meaningful once again. Shortly afterwards, she met another man, Ray, who promised to take care of her. This time, she was very cautious and careful. He appeared promising but she believed nothing he told her. He was from Ivory Coast. He showered Emma and Joy with love and affection, reassuring Emma his relationship with her would be different. As time went on, Emma grew to trust him. She believed him because he loved her daughter so much.

But unfortunately, trouble started again for Emma when Ray's family refused to allow him to settle down with Emma. They insisted he marry someone from their country, because of a bitter experience he had gone through in the hands of a Cameroonian in the past. No matter how Ray tried to persuade them, they resented Emma. When they discovered she was pregnant with his child they threatened to kill her. Emma ran to her church for help. She hid there with Joy for months, hoping the church would be able to make peace with Ray's family. Several attempts were made by elders of the church to talk to them but all their efforts fell on deaf ears. At some point, the life of the pastor of the church was also threatened, and, the church felt it was better for Emma to leave the country. The church gave her some money, which she added to her savings. She was introduced to an agent who specialised in helping people abroad. Emma's savings could barely cover her trip so she decided to leave her daughter in the custody of the elders of her church. The agent got Emma an international passport and a ticket. A few weeks later, Emma came to Ireland.

Zimbabwe at a Glance

History: Popularly called the home of the Victoria Falls and regarded as one of the natural wonders of the world, Zimbabwe is a developing landlocked country in the southern part of Africa. The word 'Zimbabwe' is derived from Shona words meaning 'houses of stone' or 'venerated house'. Zimbabwe is bordered by Botswana to the west, Zambia to the north, Mozambique to the east and South Africa to the south. The capital city of Zimbabwe is Harare. Bantu-speaking farmers, known as Khoisan settlers or Iron Age migrants from the north, were the first occupants of the Great Zimbabwe site in the south of the country. The first British explorers, colonists, European gold seekers, ivory hunters and missionaries arrived in Zimbabwe in the 1850s, and the massive influx of foreigners later led to the establishment of the territory Rhodesia, named after Cecil Rhodes of the British South African Company. In 1923, European settlers voted to become the self-governing British colony of Southern Rhodesia. For much of the last half-century Zimbabwe's history has been that of the long struggle to end white rule. Conflicts between black and white came into sharp focus because of the ownership of the best farmland by skilled traders and professionals. This forced Africans to work on white farms, in mines and in factories. Poor wages and conditions led to rebellion and African political parties emerged.

Ian Smith became Rhodesia's president in 1964. In November 1965, the conservative white-minority government of Rhodesia declared its independence from Britain but the UK did not recognise the declaration and demanded more complete voting rights for the black African majority in the country. The African parties opted for increasingly fierce guerrilla warfare. The country resisted the demands of black Africans, and Prime Minister Ian Smith withstood British pressure, economic sanctions and guerrilla attacks to uphold white supremacy. On 1 March 1970, Rhodesia formally proclaimed itself a republic. Smith tried ceasefires, amnesties, secret talks and sneaky assassinations, all of which failed to curb the fighting. Heightened guerrilla warfare and a withdrawal of South African military aid in 1976 marked the beginning of the collapse of Smith's 11 years of resistance.

Finally there was a general non-racial election and Smith was forced to hand over leadership to a man who was not taken very seriously internationally. African nations and rebel leaders immediately denounced the action, but Western governments were more reserved, although none granted recognition to the new regime. Finally, in 1979, a new constitution that provided for democratic majority rule was established. The white minority finally consented in a carefully monitored multiracial election in March 1980 that made Zimbabwe join the ranks of Africa's independent nations.

Economy: The government of Zimbabwe has faced a wide variety of difficult economic problems in its struggles to develop a market-oriented economy. Its involvement in the war in the Democratic Republic of the Congo drained hundreds of millions of dollars from the economy. Badly needed support from the IMF was suspended because of the country's failure to meet budgetary goals. Inflation rose from an annual rate of 32% in 1998, 59% in 1999, 60% in 2000 to 100% by the end of 2001. The economy is being steadily weakened by excessive government deficits, AIDS and rampant inflation. The government's land-reform programme, characterised by chaos and violence, has derailed the commercial sector, the traditional source of exports, foreign exchange, the provider of thousands of jobs and made the distribution of income extremely unequal. For years Zimbabwe has been the world's third biggest source of tobacco and is potentially a breadbasket for surrounding countries, which often depend on its food exports. Today some of the country's challenges include the need to address unresolved land issues, a rampant AIDS problem, declining respect for the law and an economic crisis. The AIDS epidemic is raging throughout southern Africa, and Zimbabwe is one of the world's worst hit countries. The pandemic is having profound effects on the country's health system, economy and development. Since the election, inflation has hit 300%, farming has been destroyed and the country faces severe food shortages. In March 2003, a brutal crackdown followed a nationwide strike. The country has in recent years moved increasingly towards a more liberal economy and the era of violent internal strife appears to have subsided.

Population: The population of Zimbabwe has been estimated to be 11,376,676, out of which 1.6 million are in its capital Harare.

Seventy-six per cent of the people are Shona, 18% Ndebele, 2% Batonka, 1% Shangaan, another 1% Venda and the remaining Asian and European.

Languages: Though English is the official language in Zimbabwe, it is a first language for only about 2% of the population. The rest are native speakers of Bantu languages, the two most prominent of which are Shona (spoken by 76%) and Sindebele (spoken by 18%). The Sindebele 'click' is made by drawing the tongue away from the front teeth, slapping it on the roof of the mouth or drawing it quickly sideways from the right upper gum.

Culture: Zimbabwe is known for traditional arts such as pottery, basketry, textiles, jewellery and carving. Most notable for their quality and beauty are the symmetrically patterned woven baskets and the stools usually carved from a single piece of wood. A few Zimbabwean sculptors are recognised among the world's best. Another tradition and culture in Zimbabwe is the prescribed punishment for certain violations, such as being forced to make a meal of one's totem animal. Zimbabwe's mesmerising music is also an important part of its cultural life. The most unusual percussion instrument used is the 'mujejeje' ('stone bells'), comprising many stones in granite outcrops around the country. It is also used in making clothes and when struck resounds with a lovely bell-like tone. (There are many ethnic groups in Zimbabwe but the major ones are the Sonas and the Ndebeles.)

Religion: Though 40–50% of Zimbabweans belong to Christian churches, their belief system is characterised more by a hybrid of traditional beliefs than by dogmatic Christianity. The Mwari cult, a monotheistic animist belief system, which entails ancestor worship, spiritual proxy and intercession, is the dominant non-Christian religion. Mwari is the unknowable supreme being that speaks to his human subjects through the voice of a cave-dwelling oracle, who is most often a female. This oracle serves as an intermediary between the spirits, the god and the people, especially in cases of natural disaster or outside aggression. In 1896 it was the oracle who received the go-ahead to begin the first rebellion (chimurenga) in Zimbabwe.

Food: The legacy of bland British fare combined with normally stodgy African dishes is Zimbabwean cuisine. The dietary staple is sadza, a white maize-meal porridge on which other local meals are built. Other delicacies are made from nyama, crocodile, kudu and impala (different kinds of meat). Chibuku, an alcoholic tipple of the masses in Zimbabwe, known as 'the beer of good cheer', is served in buckets that are passed between partakers. Chibuku, which is not very tasty, is drunk mainly in high-density township beer halls, a distinctly male social scene.

Tourist Attractions: Zimbabwe is certainly an unbeatable destination for adventure travel of all sorts. Not only are its game reserves among the most abundant and beautiful on the continent, but they also offer unusual safari experiences that are simply unavailable anywhere else. A beautiful country, Zimbabwe boasts the majestic Victoria Falls, magnificent wildlife preserves and the medieval ruins of Great Zimbabwe in the bustling city of Harare. Bequeathed a distinctly European flavour by its colonisers, Harare is Zimbabwe's showpiece city, centre of commerce, home of the national gallery of Zimbabwe, the Harare gardens and the Kopie granite hill. The north-eastern border of the country is marked by the mighty Zambezi river, along which is located the incomparable spectacle of Victoria Falls and the magnificent expanse of Lake Kariba. The Victoria Falls is the world-famous greatest attraction in Zimbabwe. Every minute an average of 550,000 cubic metres of water plummets over the edge of the falls, except at the flood stage between the months of March and May when up to 5 million cubic metres per minute pass over the falls. The Zambezi has also become one of the world's best water adventure-travel destinations in Zimbabwe, offering outstanding white-water rafting in the Zambezi gorges below the falls as well as excellent canoeing and kayaking above them. Zimbabwe is also known for Matobo, home to the world's greatest concentration of black eagles. The stone enclosures of Great Zimbabwe, which are the remnants of a past empire, and the herds of elephant and other game roaming vast stretches of wilderness are also associated with this great country.

CHAPTER TWO

Violet
Zimbabwe

Violet attempted to relax as the aircraft took off. But she just couldn't. She turned and shifted in her chair. She was disturbed, hungry, worried and tired. She tried again and again to put her thoughts behind her, at least for the trip, but the picture of her son Jude kept appearing before her. She could see the tears that ran freely down his cheeks as she handed him over to her cousin. His red swollen face, screaming protest, was all she saw before her.

Despite the fact that she was starving, Violet didn't have the appetite to eat anything. She was so worried about Jude that the hope of a new life no longer meant anything to her. It was the first time she had parted from him and she wasn't sure if she would be able to go through with it. She wasn't even sure if she would ever see him alive again. She had been left to take care of him alone since his birth and they had both been through a lot together. They had both suffered and gone through hell, and the sudden escape from it all was still unbelievable to Violet. Many times in the past she had believed that they would both end up dead. It was a miracle that they had both survived. Her son's father, Alan, had abandoned her while she was pregnant with Jude, when she discovered that he was married and had a daughter her age. That discovery was like a knife in her back and, since then, her past had haunted her everywhere she went.

Violet turned to her face the window. The beauty of Zimbabwe International Airport had no impact on her. She hid her face from the person seated next to her so he wouldn't see the sadness written on it. Her eyes were swollen shut from lack of sleep and weeping. Tears were now a part of her and she could hardly concentrate on anything any more. She had not been able to afford a decent meal for weeks before the trip. She had starved to make the trip possible and she strongly believed the decision to leave would bring a new life for her and Jude. It was by luck that Violet had stumbled on help; she had been warned she had no other choice but to make the trip – otherwise her life or her son's would be wasted. They had narrowly escaped death several times, and she knew it was just a matter of time before their luck would run out.

Violet had to flee her native land for safety. Her home had been destroyed. She had slept in the streets for several months with her son and often had been forced to run from danger in the middle of the night, dragging the little boy with her. Since Violet had lost her parents and one of her brothers, she had been left with nothing. Her other brothers had also vanished without trace after they had left home in search of greener pastures.

Violet had no home and no money. It was her mother's death that hit her most. They had been very close and Violet had spent the best part of her youth with her, until she fell ill and passed away.

As the aircraft took off, yet another picture of her father abusing her mother and his children flashed through her mind. Violet had witnessed it all. She had no good memories of her childhood and she knew that if she'd carried on the way she had, she would have either ended up insane or dead. She needed to get away from it all, to get a new life. She needed a soothing balm for her wounds and a caring hand to wipe away her tears. She wanted to experience the other side of life, to feel love rather than hatred around her. She looked out of the window of the aircraft as the clouds came up and the city disappeared before her eyes. In her heart she said goodbye to Zimbabwe, praying that the horrible things she had experienced there would fade as the city faded out of her sight.

Violet had grown up in Mapani village in Zimbabwe. Zimbabwe is located in the southern part of Africa and until the late nineties was one of the greatest African countries and a big attraction for thousands of tourists. The political and economic problems, coupled with drought, AIDS, floods and many other disasters, had contributed to the fall of the great country. Violet's parents were very poor peasant farmers. Like many others, Violet's parents had no other means of living other than their farm work. They lived and worked to survive and to feed their eight children. They planted vegetables, fruits and crops, which they ate and sold to make some money. Life was extremely difficult for them because they hardly had enough food left for sale after feeding their family, but they were content with what they had. Most times, they had just enough to eat but, all through the years, they managed to get by. Once in a while, they were lucky enough to make a little extra money. They were always happy when this happened because it meant extra food for everyone. They lived together as one happy family, sharing each other's joy and pain. Throughout their primary and secondary education, none of the children owned shoes. They walked barefoot everywhere they went. It was the nineties before Violet could afford to buy her first pair of shoes as a teenager.

On a typical school day everyone would be up as early as 3 a.m. to go to the fields, where they planted maize, cotton, wheat and groundnuts. Every day they trekked for hours to get to the farm and, besides the backbreaking work of hoeing, planting, weeding and harvesting, they also fetched water for the house and firewood for making fires for cooking. When they finished on the farm they made their way to school, which also involved walking many miles, often in times of drought. They became accustomed to this life as they grew up.

After the children left for school, Violet's mother would continue on the farm. She would gather all the crops they had got from the farm that day and put them in baskets, which were taken to the marketplace for sale. Whatever money they made was divided in two. A part was kept for the upkeep of the house and the children's education, and the other part was for emergencies or to celebrate festive seasons like Christmas. Life to them was what they could make it, and it went well for all of them until Violet's father married another woman.

It was a shock to the family and, before they could ask him why he had done it, he left them all and moved with his new wife, Efe, into another hut beside theirs. He refused to talk to any of them, and they were only allowed to see him at the instructions of Efe. Despite this, they continued to work hard on the farm. Violet's father put Efe in charge of everything. She began to control the farm and gave Violet's mother and her children only what she wanted them to have. Nine people shared what four people would normally eat. The situation became worse when Efe started having children. Violet's father abandoned her mother totally with her eight young children. He told them that Efe had come to change his life and he was sure her presence would bring good luck, good fortune and wealth.

Violet's mother suffered a lot of violence at the hands of her father for many years and, being the youngest child, Violet witnessed it all.

He not only abused her mother, he also beat and abused all of his children, except the five Efe had for him. He constantly told them he regretted having them because he considered them useless to his life.

Violet has grown up with fear and anxiety and dreads to remember the horrible experiences of the life she had as a child. Even now that she's away from it all, she's terrified she could wake up one morning and find it starting all over again. It was a life filled with violence and poverty. Violet believes the trauma she experienced could have easily killed twenty strong people. The only good memories she has are of her early childhood days, before the nightmare began.

After her father married Efe, he called his children one day and declared that primary education was the best he could offer them, and if any of them wanted to go any further in their studies, that was their choice. The children began to struggle with their mother to save extra money to further their education. They went out daily in search of odd jobs. Three of Violet's brothers left the house in search of a better life. They never returned home. Efforts were made to trace their whereabouts but no one ever heard from them or saw them again.

For several months, a dark cloud hung over the family as they waited patiently, hoping for the best. Days went into weeks and weeks into months, but nothing happened. Being the youngest child, Violet was always left at home with her mother. She continued to help on the farm her mother had set up for herself. Luck came and hopes were renewed when one of Violet's sisters, Rose, got a grant from the Christian missionaries to go to a secondary school. The help she got encouraged Rose to plan her future. Rose sailed through school without hitch and got a job afterwards. She was determined to make and save money so she could further her education as well as help her mother and other siblings.

With her job, Rose sent Violet and three of her brothers to secondary schools. This encouraged them to be determined to make it in life.

After their secondary education, one after the other, Violet and her brothers searched for something to do. Two of them got odd jobs and the eldest one enlisted in the army. The new change in the family brought hope to Violet's mother, whose health had deteriorated. She was very happy and hopeful that the turn in her children's life would end her suffering. She particularly relied on her son in the army because he was the most favoured.

Things started to improve gradually. Two years after Violet finished her secondary education, in 1994, she got a short contract job in a bank as a clerk. The job was the best thing that could have happened to her because it offered her the opportunity to buy and own her first pair of shoes. Between 1994 and 2000 Violet worked, on and off, every time she was called back to renew her contract. She saved money from her little salary and, when she had saved something substantial, she decided to try her hand at trading. She traded in used and fairly new clothes, which she bought from Botswana, a neighbouring country to Zimbabwe. Trading conditions were not the best but she kept on, determined to survive. Most times, she slaved in the sun for several hours before she could get good bargains from her suppliers. Sometimes, she had to risk making money deposits to traders she didn't know so she could get the best when their goods arrived. She had to take care of her mother, who was much less active and gradually becoming weak. One day something happened which opened a new chapter in Violet's life. While at work one morning, one of the bank's best clients expressed his interest in her. Itayi was well known and one of the most admired clients because of the gifts he occasionally showered on the staff of the bank. He was friendly with almost everyone although no one knew much about him, apart from the fact that he kept a good account with the Bank. Violet was excited about his proposal and particularly happy when he told her he was single, hardworking and industrious. Violet's mother was happy and strongly encouraged her daughter. Violet was happy that her financial worries would come to an end. Itayi was nice, loving and promising, and this made her grow fond of him.

Disaster struck in 1997 when Violet found out, at the same time she discovered she was pregnant, that he was married with four daughters and two sons. The worst came when she also discovered his first daughter was the same age as her. About the same time, Itayi's wife found out about her and sent threatening messages to her. It was a horrible blow to Violet. She was shocked and devastated. Her mother and brothers were so bitter that they vowed to maim Itayi if they ever saw him near their house again. Violet blamed herself for it all. She had been carried away by the gifts he showered on her. She didn't know what to do. She wanted nothing to do with him but she felt she would be foolish to send him away. She needed money and support. She didn't believe in abortions, nor did she believe in having a baby without a father. She was confused. They continued to see each other, but this soon became difficult for Violet because nobody around her would accept him. Itayi's wife continued to send threatening messages to her. A few months later, Itayi left Violet. He abandoned her with the pregnancy and made no effort to see her ever again.

News came to Violet's mother that her son, who fought for liberation as an army officer, had died. Rumours went round that agents working for the government had killed him. The family went into mourning and Violet's father swore to find and deal with the people who had killed his son. He went around accusing anyone he suspected and openly challenged the government to deny they were responsible for his son's death. He went to gatherings and meeting he wasn't invited to, to protest his son's death. He made enemies. Anonymous warnings were sent to him to desist and forget the past, but he refused. After several months, Violet's father was kidnapped and killed and his body dumped in the bush. His family reported the crime when they discovered his body. Nothing was done and no investigations were made into his death. His family and neighbours were scared of talking about it in case they were the next to go. In one of the daily newspapers, a doctor was quoted as saying Violet's father had died of a heart attack but no one believed it. The shock was too much for Violet's mother. It affected her so much that she lost hope for everything in life. Her illness became worse. She developed high blood pressure, collapsed and had a stroke. She prayed to die rather than suffer but death never came. She became very sad, crying constantly, asking herself why after working so hard she had been neglected by her husband, lost a son with two still missing, and was paralysed and bed ridden with no help or medication. She blamed herself. She blamed her late husband. She blamed life.

Violet watched her mother's health deteriorate as her own pregnancy grew. Neither of them got any medical attention, despite their conditions. She knew there was nothing she could do except to work harder and pray for the situation to improve. Each time her mother tried to talk, Violet knew she was trying to tell her something very important. Violet continued to work, even when she was weak and hardly able to carry on. Her mother's situation became worse and, when she could no longer cope with taking care of her, she arranged for her to be taken to a hospital. She put down all her savings for her mother's medical bill and went back to Botswana to trade. She continued to trade in used clothes. She slept in the street at night until she returned to Zimbabwe.

One Saturday, in 1998, just three days after Violet returned from a trip to Botswana, she was rushed to the hospital and after a few hours she had a baby boy. Rather than being happy, she was very sad and depressed. She had no idea how she was going to cope with taking care of herself, the baby and her sick mother. She tried to seek help from friends, neighbours and family members but she received none. Two days after her son was born, Violet put together all the money she had saved and headed for Botswana to continue trading. With the baby strapped to her back, she shuttled between Botswana and Zimbabwe at least three days a week to trade. She had no good clothes or nappies for her son. He looked emaciated. Apart from breast milk, he got nothing else. It was really bad and Violet prayed to survive the trauma.

She intensified her efforts by going from house to house and begging people to buy the second-hand clothes she sold. At the end of each day, she slept with tramps and the destitute in the streets, or anywhere she could find that was comfortable enough. She did this three days a week and on the fourth day she would be back on the bus to do a twelve-hour trip to Zimbabwe. The little money she made went into taking care of her mother and son. This went on for weeks, which ran into months and then into years. Violet was just barely able to survive by this means.

In 1999 Violet's mother died. Even though Violet had expected it, she still lost everything. Her plans, joy, happiness and everything she hoped for went with her mother's death. She was left alone in the house. She became depressed.

After weeks of crying her eyes out, she was back on her trips to Botswana. Determined to survive, she wanted to do more to make more money. In addition to trading, she went from house to house washing and ironing clothes. At night, she was back on the streets.

Most times throughout the night, her eyes would be wide open, and though she was always tired and wanted to sleep, her eyelids just wouldn't close. Sometimes it was stress related and sometimes it was due to fear that she and her baby would be kidnapped or killed. It was a miracle that her son survived.

On one of her trips back home, Violet discovered the hut that served as her house had been ransacked and destroyed. All her valuables and the little money she had saved had been stolen. Life came to a standstill for her and, this time, she felt like taking her son's life and hers. She believed that if she took only her own life he would be left to suffer alone. She cried to her neighbours. No one was willing to give her details of what had happened. Rumours went round that she had been accused of being an active member of a new political party, the Movement Democratic Party, that was against the activities of the government. It was believed that she had joined the party to train in the army to fight the government and avenge the death of her brother and father. Violet did no such thing and had no such plans.

Government loyalists searched for people they believed were part of the new political party and dealt severely with them. People were captured daily and they vanished without trace. Most of the kidnappings were done at night and those kidnapped were thrown into the back of vans and driven away to unknown destinations. Often villagers peeped from behind their curtains and watched the vans being driven away. No one said anything. No one wanted to talk or associate with people who were labelled enemies of the government. Violet was threatened many times that she would disappear like the others if she didn't desist from her secret plans so it came as no surprise when she began to have problems with her neighbours and the villagers. They made life difficult for her and avoided her. She was regarded as an outcast and no one wanted to have anything to do with her. She went into hiding until she finally left for Botswana with her son, who was just a few months old. She lived on the streets. She shared dilapidated and uncompleted buildings with the destitute and the homeless. She continued to wash and iron for people and still managed to save something out of what she made. She remained in Botswana for years, begging everyone she could for help. Eventually she met a wealthy trader who promised to help her out of the country to a better place if she could save enough money.

With determination Violet set out to meet her target. She took up extra work and slaved for two years, between 1999 and 2001. When she had saved something substantial, she went back to Zimbabwe and obtained an international passport.

Violet left the shores of Zimbabwe for Ireland in 2001, painfully leaving her son behind with her cousin because she could not afford to pay for his trip. Two days after she came to Ireland, she got a sales job and, after saving for six months, she sent for her son who now lives with her.

Democratic Republic of Congo at a Glance

History: Formerly known as the Belgian Congo, this territory was inhabited by ancient Negrito peoples (pygmies) who were pushed into the mountains by Bantu and Nilotic invaders decades ago. The American correspondent Henry M. Stanley navigated the Congo river in 1877 and opened the interior to exploration. Commissioned by King Leopold II of the Belgians, Stanley made treaties with native chiefs. This enabled the king to obtain personal title to the territory at the Berlin Conference of 1885. Leopold accumulated a vast personal fortune from ivory and rubber through Congolese slave labour and 10 million people were estimated to have died from forced labour, starvation and outright extermination during his colonial rule. His brutal exploitation of the Congo eventually became an international cause célèbre, prompting Belgium to take over the administration of the Congo, which remained a colony until agitation for independence forced Brussels to grant freedom to the republic in 1960. In elections after independence, prominent nationalist Patrice Lumumba became the prime minister while Joseph Kasavubu became head of state, but within weeks of independence the Katanga Province, led by Moise Tshombe, seceded from the new republic, followed shortly by another mining province, South Kasai. This led to civil war. Belgium sent paratroopers to quell the war and the United Nations flew in a peacekeeping force. Kasavubu staged an army coup in 1960 and handed Lumumba over to the Katangan forces. A UN investigating commission found that Lumumba had been killed by a Belgian mercenary in the presence of Tshombe, who was then the president of Katanga. Kasavubu abruptly dismissed Tshombe from the coalition government in 1965 but was himself ousted by General Joseph-Desiré Mobutu, an army chief of staff. The new president nationalised the 'Union Minière', the Belgian copper-mining enterprise that had been a dominant force in the Congo since colonial days. In 1975, he nationalised much of the economy, barred religious instruction in schools and decreed the adoption of African names. He changed the country's name to Zaire and his own to Mobuto Sese Seko, which means 'the all-powerful warrior who because of his endurance and inflexible will to win will go from conquest to conquest leaving fire in his wake'. In 1977, invaders from Angola calling themselves the Congolese National Liberation Front pushed into Shaba and threatened the important mining centre of Kolwezi. France and Belgium provided military aid to defeat these rebels. Laurent Kabila and his long-standing but little-known guerrilla movement launched a seven-month campaign that ousted Mobutu in May 1997, ending his regime. Mobutu fled in exile to Morocco on 16 May 1997 where he died of cancer in September.

The country was then renamed the Democratic Republic of the Congo, its name before Mobutu changed it to Zaire in 1971. But elation over Mobutu's downfall faded as Kabila's own autocratic style emerged and he seemed devoid of a clear plan for reconstructing the country. In August 1998, Congolese rebel forces led by ethnic Tutsi in eastern Congo and backed by Rwanda and Uganda began attacking Kabila's forces. The rebels gained control of a large portion of the country until Angolan, Namibian and Zimbabwean troops came to Kabila's aid and pushed them back. On 16 January 2001, Kabila was assassinated by one of his bodyguards and his son Joseph was named head of state ten days later. The new president demonstrated a willingness to engage in talks to end the civil war. In April 2002, the government agreed to a power-sharing arrangement with Ugandan-supported rebels and in July of the same year the presidents of both Congo and Rwanda signed an accord. Rwanda promised to withdraw its 35,000 troops from the eastern Congolese border while the Congo agreed to disarm the thousands of Hutu militiamen in its territory. In September 2002, Uganda also signed a peace accord with the nation, though the warring parties were slow to depart. Most of them had been looting the Congo of its natural resources and had little incentive to end the war. More than 2.5 million people died in the Congo's complex four-year civil war, which involved seven foreign armies and numerous rebel groups that often fought among themselves. Despite the peace agreement and power-sharing plan signed between the main parties in the four-year war, the fighting and killing continued into 2003. In April 2003, hundreds of civilians were massacred in the eastern province of Ituri in an ethnic conflict and in June of the same year a French force with a UN mandate was deployed to defend the population from further tribal fighting.

Economy: The economy of the Democratic Republic of the Congo, a nation endowed with vast potential wealth, has declined drastically since the mid eighties. The war, which began in August 1998, has dramatically reduced the national output and the revenue of the government has increased external debt. Foreign businesses have curtailed operations due to uncertainty about the outcome of the conflict, lack of infrastructure, and the difficult operating environment. The war has intensified the impact of such basic problems as an uncertain legal framework, corruption, raging inflation and a lack of openness in government economic policy and financial operations. A number of International Monetary Fund (IMF) and World Bank missions have met with the government to help it develop a coherent economic plan.

Population: The population of the republic of Congo is estimated to be 55,225,478. About one million refugees fled into the republic in 1994 as a result of the ethnic fighting in Rwanda. Later fighting between rebels and government forces in 1996 caused not less than 875,000 refugees already in the republic to return to Rwanda. In addition the regional war in the republic in August 1998 left 1.8 million Congolese displaced and caused another 300,000 Congolese refugees to flee to surrounding countries.

Languages: The languages spoken in the republic of Congo are French (official), Lingala (a lingua franca trade language), Kingwana (a dialect of Kiswahili or Swahili), Kikongo and Tshiluba.

Culture: Surviving national folk traditions in Congo are evident in pottery and the weaving of raffia. They are also present in ceremonial dresses and costumes for dancing and in songs. Congolese still create such traditional objects as masks, figures, stones and nail-studded statues. Congo's unique popular music mixes traditional rhythms and instruments borrowed from other cultures, civilisations and continents. Congolese music, which is popular all over Africa, has given birth to a great variety of dance steps and styles.

Ethnic groups: The ethnic groups in Congo are Kongo 48%, Sangha 20%, M'Bochi 12%, Teke 17%, and the Europeans less than 1%. Religions: In the republic of Congo the Roman Catholics make up 50%, the Protestants 20%, the Kimbanguists 10%, Muslims 10%, other syncretic sects and indigenous beliefs make up the remaining 10%.

Food: Typical Congolese meals consist of any starchy food with sauce or stew. Cassava is the principal starch, particularly in rural areas, and it may be replaced by rice or corn if they are available. These basic foods are served mostly with thick stew or porridge flavoured with a spicy sauce. If affordable, fish or meat may be added to the stew. At meals a bowl of cassava or rice and a bowl of stew are placed on the ground or a table, and the family gathers around. Each person takes a handful of the rice or other staple and mixes it with some sauce to form a ball. Although food is often left unseasoned, many Congolese cooks spice their stews with pepper. The basic stew is called mwamba and is made with chicken, beef, fish or lamb, browned in oil before stewing. It is eaten with rice, fufu (cornflour dough) or chikwange (cassava prepared in banana leaves). Those who eat breakfast usually have café au lait and a slice of French baguette. The main meal, traditionally eaten at midday, is now more usually eaten in the evening. Other common dishes include pili pili chicken, maboke (freshwater fish cooked in leaves) and saka saka. Congolese cooks like to prepare the entire meal in one pot to save on fuel.

Tourist Attraction: In Congo the rainforests filled with okoume, limba and other trees, as well as the plateaus of the savanna, which support jackals, hyenas, cheetahs, antelope, monkeys, elephants, wild boar and giraffes, all seem to say 'this is Africa'. Kinshasa, the capital of Congo, does not have many sights of historic interest but the prehistoric and ethnological museums at Kinshasa University, an ensemble of light, rectangular, well laid-out buildings standing on a hillside, are worth seeing. A brightly coloured chapel crowns the top of the hill. Other attractions include the fishing port of Kinkole, the gardens of the Presidential Farm of Nsele, made of pagodas, and the extensive pools where angling and swimming may be enjoyed. Also worth seeing in the markets and suburbs of Kinshasa are craftsmen who produce wood and metal items.

Kasai & Sha: In the south of the country, the Upemba National Park straddles the popular river Lualaba. It also includes several lakes inhabited by hippos, crocodiles and numerous aquatic birds. Here too are fishermen, cattle farmers and peasants, as well as a number of mining communities. The whole of the south is dotted with freshwater lakes such as Munkamba, Fwa and Kasai and there are also numerous impressive waterfalls such as Kiobo on river Lufira and Lofol, 1,259 feet high, in the north of Lubumbashi.

Upper Congo & the Kiv: The high plateaux of Congo extend across the eastern part of the country around lakes Tanganyika, Kivu, Edward, Albert and Bukavu. In the north is the Garamba National Park, covering 400,000 hectares and featuring lions, leopards, elephants, rhinos and giraffes. Lake Albert, which contains more fish than any other lake in Africa, lies at an altitude of over 2,027 feet. It can be reached from Bunia, which is also the point of departure for numerous excursions into the forests and mountains, the native villages, the Caves of Mount Hoyo and the Escaliers de Venus Falls. Lake Edward is the home of birds of all sizes and colours. The mountain scenery between Goma and Beni is regarded as some of the most spectacular in Africa.

Virunga National Park: Covering an area of 12,000 square kilometres (4,633 square miles), this park comprises an immense plain bounded by two jagged mountain ranges that serve as a natural enclosure for the animals that roam at liberty in this huge natural reserve. The game includes numerous lions, elephants, buffalos, warthogs, antelopes, hippos and colourful aquatic birds. In this park it is possible to climb the still active volcanoes of Nyamuragira and Nyiragongo.

Southwest Congo & Bandundu: The Insiki Falls, which are 197 feet high, at Zongo and the caves in the region of Mbanza-Ngungu are pleasant resorts. Close to the Mbanza-Ngungu area is Frère Gillet Botanic Gardens in Kisantu, with its world-famous rare orchids. Further west are the wild slopes and gorges of the River Kwilu and on the right bank of the river is a spot of rugged beauty called Inga. Less easily accessible is the upper valley of the Kwango in the southwest and a long journey through a region of unspoiled natural beauty leads to the Tembo (formerly Guillaume) Falls.

CHAPTER THREE

Lydia
Democratic Republic of Congo

The sun shone on the field giving it a glassy look. The weather was particularly warm in Ireland that morning. Young women, men, children and the old lazed in the field, chattering away. It was a beautiful day and the different colours of their robes made it more beautiful. The sea next to the field was calm. A child ran across the field. His mother followed shortly after, and everyone laughed. Lydia watched as her neighbours had fun. She wanted to be part of it, but she couldn't brush aside the thoughts that flooded her mind. The little boy ran past her again. The beach faded from her eyes as her mind drifted off. She was no longer with the crowd. She was far away in her country, the Democratic Republic of Congo, hidden in a deserted camp.

Someone nudged her, breaking her chain of thought. It was her husband, Ron. Lydia looked into his eyes. For the first time in many months she smiled with relief. She was glad she had him. She was glad they were alive. She was glad she was safe from the clutches of death. She was glad she could roam the fields without a gun being pointed at her. She was glad she could practise her profession with ease. She was glad about so many things. Everything seemed to be just right.

Sitting down beside her husband, she stretched her legs under the scorching sun. He was saying something about the beauty of the surroundings but she hardly heard him. She just smiled and nodded her head in agreement as she rolled a ball in her hands. Her thoughts hit her in small flashes and she realised that she just needed to put one foot in front of the other until time healed her wounds. She knew she had to move on, to bury the past and plan for the future. She no longer needed to hide from anyone. She had the opportunity to improve her work skills. There were good prospects for the future. Though the system, people and food were different here, she was quick to adjust and blend in. She was ready to make the best of her new home. Unlike most of her colleagues, language was not a barrier for her. She was fluent in two major languages, English and French, which are spoken in most countries around the world. Though she was glad to be free at last, she missed the job and the colleagues she had left behind. They had shared so many things together.

Lydia shook her head at a chocolate bar her husband offered her. She looked around. More people had joined them. She threw a ball and her husband made a run for it. With all the ugly thoughts behind her, Lydia began to plan her future. She patted her stomach and her baby kicked. She was sure it was in protest at what had happened to her. She needed her baby's love and support as much as the baby needed hers. Her daily activities and immediate plans centred on the arrival of the baby. It was her first and the excitement was almost unbearable. The dawn of each day drew her closer to the arrival of her joy. The happiness this brought to her drowned the sorrow of the past. Throwing her scarf over her shoulders, she went in search of her husband.

When Lydia was a child, her father was a businessman who sold car wheels. As his business thrived, he also thrived. His network grew to most parts of Europe and when the opportunity came for him to work in Belgium he did not decline the offer. Lydia's mother traded in landed properties, buying and re-selling to the rich and powerful in the country. At that time, not many people were involved in the land business and she was one of the few who knew the tricks of the trade. She made money and, with it, invested in the future of her children.

Being the last of the children and the only one not in school, Lydia's father took her with him to Belgium, where his business often took him. He had arranged one of the best schools for her. She was going to start her primary education there. Lydia cried her eyes out. She pleaded with her mother to stop her father from taking her away. She was too young to understand why she was singled out and why her father had to take her away from her brothers and sisters.

For the first few weeks she spent in Belgium, she refused to mix with other children but, when her new environment offered her more excitement, she swiftly changed her mind. It didn't take long before the memories of her friends in Congo faded away. Gradually, the picture of her home also faded from her eyes. She began to bond with her schoolmates. She particularly enjoyed treking to school with two other children who lived in her neighbourhood. She was the only black child in the neighbourhood and in her class but she mixed very well. She never noticed her colour was different. She was not treated differently or reminded that she had a different skin colour from the others. Because she was new in her class, everyone vied for her attention, and she loved being the centre of attraction. She looked forward to each day in school. It came as a shock when her father informed her he was withdrawing her from school to take her back to Congo. His contract had ended and he had to return home. Lydia refused to leave. Like music being replayed, she cried her eyes out again when her father withdrew her from school and took her back to Congo. In Congo, she completed her primary education. The time she had spent in Belgium had built a lot of confidence in her. It had served as a good foundation for her education. The system of education in Congo was a bit different from that of Belgium. Lydia sometimes found herself operating on a different level to her classmates. She soon adapted. Within a few months of her return, she had adjusted to the system. She came top of her class and excelled.

After her primary education she went to one of the best secondary schools in Kinshasa. It was a whole new experience for her again. Apart from the usual academic work, the school offered many other activities such as sports, music, drama and traditional dancing. All these came with their own fun and excitement, and Lydia participated in most of them. She was brilliant. She was chosen to regularly represent her school in various inter-school competitions. Different schools came together regularly for debates and other competitions to determine what school was the best in the country at the end of every year. Awards were given to such schools. Students were proud to be associated with these schools. It was an experience Lydia enjoyed. The debating class was her favourite because, though shy, she was very outspoken and could express herself very well. Her diction was quite different from that of the others and she spoke with the expressions and phonetics she had learned in Belgium. Every clap or cheer from the audience built her confidence, and this encouraged her to enter as many competitions as she could. Another activity she involved herself in was dancing. She participated in traditional dancing, which involved drumming and dancing, using traditional instruments. She was also on the handball team. Her excellent performance in science subjects encouraged her to go for a profession in the health sector. By the time she was in her last year, she had chosen to study medicine and she worked towards achieving this goal.

Studying medicine at the university was another exciting experience for Lydia. She was young and full of life but inexperienced. She was very shy. There were challenges to be faced, work to be done and targets to be met. It was tough. At first, she called her parents at every opportunity for help and advice when she faced difficult issues. But, later, she learnt that if she didn't help herself, no one else would. The anatomy part of the course took her a long time to come to terms with. Seeing and dissecting dead bodies, mutilated body parts and the human brain were a nightmare to her. She dreaded every anatomy class and for a long time she couldn't eat anything with her bare hands. Every time she remembered a dead face, she wept.

Apart from that she was happy. She hardly lacked anything. Her parents provided her with everything she wanted. Many times she wanted to return home and change her course of study but her father always told her to face whatever came her way with a bold heart. He always assured her that, with time, she would get used to it. 'Every pain and every joy means progress' was her mother's favourite saying, which Lydia wrote on a piece of paper and stuck on the wall of her room. Any time she was down, she read it over and over and drew strength from it. The obstacles and challenges came and, one by one, Lydia tackled and overcame them. By the time she was in her third year in the university, her entire life had changed. She was a different person with goals and ideals. At the end of her course she achieved excellent grades.

After her studies, Lydia began to search for a job. The jaws of a shaky and poor economy bit hard into the fabric of the society. The political unrest gave birth to a war and a lot of people fled the country as a result.

As with most conflicts in Africa, the situation in the Democratic Republic of Congo had much to do with the legacy of colonialism. It all started with the violent 1885 Belgian imposition of colonial rule in Congo. Millions were killed. The murders were grotesque, with chopped limbs and many horrible sights. After 75 years of colonial rule, the Belgians left very abruptly in 1960, relinquishing the political rights to the people of Congo. However, economic rights were not there to enable the country to flourish. The country began to experience traces of unrest in the nineties and the poor economic situation, which fuelled the unrest, led to a conflict that involved many nations. The country became hell. Fighting was fuelled by the country's vast mineral wealth. This led to a war which had an economic as well as a political side to it. The war centred mainly in eastern Congo, involved nine other African nations and directly affected the lives of at least 50 million Congolese. Described by some as Africa's First World War, the war in the Democratic Republic of the Congo (DRC) was the widest interstate war in modern African history.

It began in 1998, when rebels supported by Uganda and Rwanda took control of several key border towns in eastern Congo and began pushing towards the capital, Kinshasa. Along the line, Angola and Zimbabwe jumped into the game, bolstering the head of state's forces with guns and soldiers. In addition to this, the rebels fighting the governments of Rwanda, Burundi and Uganda pursued by government troops from their countries made the Democratic Republic of Congo their base. The ensuing years of bloodshed left Congo's security situation unstable and its already inadequate infrastructure in shambles. An estimated 2.5 million people were believed to have died because of the conflict. For over two years the United Nations peacekeepers and local militia groups kept the peace process moving, but obstacles remained with opposing sides proving difficult. The continued presence of Ugandan troops in the Democratic Republic of Congo had less to do with the weeding out of Ugandan rebels, as claimed, and more with plundering the country's diamond, gold and timber resources. Rival rebel groups fought for control of the country's lucrative tantalite deposits, an important mineral used in making mobile phones. The problems in the republic led non-governmental organisations to label the situation the worst humanitarian crisis in the world, with 16 million people suffering from severe famine and two million displaced from their homes. Thousands crossed the border to Rwanda.

Lydia worked as a medical doctor at that time. The distress the country was going through affected a lot of professionals. What Lydia detested most was the state of the hospital where she worked. Considered one of the best hospitals in Congo, it was in fact old, underequipped and under-staffed. The poor economic situation made equipment for the hospital very difficult to get. The old equipment had been in use for decades and needed to be replaced. It was either too outdated or no longer functional because of lack of maintenance. Many patients whose lives could have been saved had died from mere carelessness or lack of basic requirements in the hospital. The situation was very bad. The salaries paid in the health sector were poor and this made the living and working conditions for health personnel sometimes unbearable.

For a long time, Lydia was faced with the problem of constantly working overtime or working on her days off. The number of staff that worked in the hospital was a third of what was required. The living conditions for the medical personnel were very poor. It was so bad that some of them could barely cater for their families. In the middle of it all, Lydia got married to Ron, a medical doctor who worked in the hospital with her.

Lydia's job became more demanding. Diseases had spread like wildfire and hundreds of people had been hospitalised. Several hospitals and private clinics were raided daily by rebels, as there was a constant search for top government dignitaries who were on admission. Rebels maimed people at will and threatened to deal with any hospital that dared to treat or admit these dignitaries. Lydia and many other doctors were persecuted. They were stopped, harassed and threatened wherever they went. Many of them moved from their houses and hid where they could not be traced. Lydia and Ron had been hopping from one friend's house to the other since the unrest began. Her parents could not help. Their lives were also at risk but they knew Lydia was in a lot more danger. They encouraged her to go into hiding because doctors especially were targets for the rebels.

On one particular occasion, Lydia narrowly escaped being killed. She had received a phone call early one morning from one of her friends, Lucy, who had promised to get her a safe place where she could stay with her husband until the situation in the country came under control. Lucy was also a medical doctor. Her father was a top government official in Congo and had a couple of guesthouses where he received his important guests. Lucy offered to house Lydia, her husband and some of their colleagues in one of the guesthouses owned by her father. It was situated away from the troubled areas. The plan was to find a temporarily safe place for them to stay while they made alternative and more solid arrangements for a more secure place.

The phone call that morning was expected, and Lydia was glad when Lucy insisted she come over. Lydia headed for her friend's house. She looked over her shoulders to be sure she was not being followed. Satisfied that she was alone, she walked briskly along a footpath to another street. Out in the open, she heaved a sigh of relief and, making the sign of the cross on her forehead, she stopped the first available bus that approached her.

Lucy's father's guesthouse, which was fenced all round, stood on its own in a newly developed area still covered with bushes and shrubs. The guesthouse had no neighbours. Lucy's father had gone into hiding since the inception of the unrest. He was very particular about the security of his properties.

Fear gripped Lydia as she approached the guesthouse. As soon as she stepped into the compound she sensed danger. The gate, which was usually locked, was wide open and the silence around the place was unusual. The gateman was missing and there was no sign of him in the small shed that he used. Lydia tiptoed to the back of the guesthouse. She heard a sound as if someone was sobbing. She paused and listened. Nothing happened for a while. But, just when she decided to move, she heard a loud thud. Her heart raced and she pressed herself against the wall of the house. Then she heard voices. Two men barked at Lucy and threatened to kill her if she did not reveal her father's hiding place to them. Lydia removed her shoes and quietly walked to the window. Carefully concealing herself, she peeped through it and almost screamed at what she saw. Lucy's hands were tied to the back of a chair. She had been stripped naked and the only covering on her was her underwear. There were whip marks all over her body. Her legs were apart, each one tied to the leg of the chair. Blood trickled down her thighs. A piece of rag gagged her mouth. She was pale, weak and tired. Tears rolled down her cheeks as she looked at the men with pleading eyes. Lydia was shocked beyond words. Her hands and body shook and she almost gave herself away. Still unsure of what to do, she listened. One of the men told the other that if by that night Lucy refused to give them the information they needed, he would eliminate her and get rid of her body.

Lydia froze. The shoes in her hand almost dropped. She tried to calm herself. Quietly, she made her way out of the compound and, as soon as she was out in the open, she ran as fast as she could. A few hours later, she was back with policemen. Lucy was rescued and saved from the murderers.

More violence erupted in the weeks that followed. Patients and workers were kidnapped from many hospitals and clinics. Tens of thousands of terrified people fled the city. Despite a peace agreement and power-sharing plan signed between the main parties in the four-year Congolese war, the fighting and killing continued. Hundreds of civilians were massacred in the eastern province in an ethnic conflict. A French force with a United Nations mandate had to be deployed to defend the population from further tribal fighting. Despite the presence of UN peacekeepers, there was a prevailing sense of insecurity. Thousands of people fled from their homes to live in camps for the internally displaced.

A large cluster of intellectuals and professionals found themselves being forced to flee the repressive measures that were imposed by the government. On many occasions, they were forced to obey rebels who went around threatening people with arms and ammunition. Many professionals were detained and tortured by rebels. The government, because of lack of trust, sacked others from their jobs. It was ironic. The professionals ran away from the rebels but the government believed they were on the side of the rebels.

Lydia and many others refused to sing to the tune of the rebels despite the fact that they feared being maimed.

When things became unbearable for them, many left their homes for camps. Lydia and her husband, Ron, left for a camp. Though several homes and buildings had been damaged by brutal tribal fighting in the area, the camp was in a remote part where they felt safe from prying eyes.

The camp was situated in a terrible area surrounded by a thick forest, which served as home to snakes and other dreadful and dangerous insects. For many months no one in Lydia's family knew where she was. There was a feeling of despair and anguish; no one knew what was going to happen to them. They shared and managed what was available. Some of them had left their homes in such a hurry that they had no change of clothes. Others were lucky to leave with substantial things, which they were glad to share with others. From time to time, a few people came around and sneaked in food and clothes to them. The war continued, claiming many lives. Some lives were lost as a direct result of the fighting. Others were lost because of various diseases and malnutrition that had spread throughout the country. The situation was the worst emergency to unfold in Africa in decades. Despite the presence of a large UN peacekeeping force, violence continued. Sometimes the UN peacekeepers themselves were targets; some were killed. Many women watched as their children died in their arms. Most of these women died soon after, not because of the conflict but mostly from diseases and starvation. More than two million people were driven from their homes, many of them beyond the reach of humanitarian agencies. A lot of people fled abroad as soon as an opportunity presented itself.

Lydia and hundreds continued to flee whenever they sensed danger. At some point, they left for Bunia, in the Ituri Region of the eastern part of Democratic Republic of Congo, near the Ugandan border.

Getting to Bunia was not easy. They flew from Kinshasa to Kisangani, in the middle of the country. From there they took another plane across the border to Entebbe in Uganda. At this stage they were faced with the only option of travelling across a lake. Lydia and Ron, like many others, were scared but they knew they had no choice. Some broke down and refused to continue the journey while others decided to brave it. From Entebbe, they took a small Ukrainian puddle-jumper across the lake. The journey took several days.

At this stage, Lydia began to make several phone calls to contact her friends in other African countries as well as those abroad. After several weeks, a few of her friends contributed some money to help her. The money came at the time she needed it most. Lydia and Ron sought help. They met Albert by a stroke of luck. Albert was a trader. His business took him to different parts of Africa and he was just passing through Bunia. He was helpful. An agreement was reached and Lydia gave him some money. He made travel arrangements and got Lydia and Ron out of Bunia within a few days to South Africa.

In South Africa, Albert got Lydia and Ron a temporary place to stay while he sorted their papers. They paid him more money. When their papers were sorted, he got them international passports and tickets. Two months later, Lydia and Ron left the shores of South Africa for Ireland.

Nigeria at a Glance

History: The earliest people that settled in Nigeria were the skilled artisans or Nok people, who had virtually disappeared by the beginning of the second millennium, after which a state known as Kanem to the north-east of Lake Chad began to flourish. Much of the state was Islamic, as were the other kingdoms around the north, and by the 14th and 15th century the southern states were dominated by a number of Yoruba empires with traditional Obas (kings). By the end of the 18th century, religious zealots in the northern part, sick of being dominated by other Islamic states, took over and created the single Islamic state of 'Sokoto' Caliphate. After that the Portuguese and the British began trading in the human misery of slaves, which was banned by 1807. After the ban, the British began to control the mines, relying heavily on mining exports at the expense of Nigeria's export food crops.

Nigeria, often regarded as the Giant of Africa, declared independence from the British on 1 October 1960. At the event the Union Jack flag was lowered for the raising of the Nigerian green, white and green flag. There were historical conflicts between the north and the south and other inter-regional fighting which made the idea of a unified republic unworkable. By 1966, the dream of a flourishing democracy was floundering amidst a series of massacres, inter-regional hostilities and finally a military coup that installed the first of a series of military governments. The Ibos in the eastern part of the country responded by seceding from the federation and declaring the independent Republic of Biafra, which started an all out civil war that lasted for nearly three years before the federal government of Nigeria won and reintegrated Biafra. The war left nearly 1,000 dead in mass destruction and famine. In 1993 the country came under an iron-fisted rule and a distinguished novelist and well-known playwright and eight others were executed for seditious political activism. The event and other despotic actions incurred the anger and condemnation of the commonwealth and other Western nations. They also sparked rioting and civil unrest across the country until 1999 when the country was free from military rule. Not long after that things started to deteriorate as several groups (religious and tribal), no longer threatened by army intervention, settled down to protracted conflict. The worst manifestation of the violence was the Sharia riots that broke out in many places in year 2000. In one night, over 300 people were killed in hand-to-hand rioting between the Ibo Christians and the Hausa Muslims in Kaduna State. The country was in turmoil and the situation was exacerbated by fuel shortages and extended power blackouts.

This original division between the Islamic government in the north and the Yoruba tribes in the south has never healed and over the years intertribal fighting and civil wars have rubbed salt into the wounds. This has extended into Nigerian politics, which up to today is riddled with tribal rivalries and ancient axes to grind. Lawlessness, widespread corruption and the lack of military control in Nigeria have allowed an almost unfettered rush of score-settling between tribes, religious groups and even rival cities.

Economy: Before oil was discovered in the late 1950s, there had been few industries and Nigeria basically survived on its agriculture for its economy and its food. Today, agriculture is still a part of the domestic economy, but by the late sixties, oil had replaced cocoa, peanuts and palm products as the country's largest foreign exchange earner. Part of the effect of the oil boom was that there was a significant rural-to-urban migration caused in part by the lure of high wages and the consumer-oriented lifestyles of the city. This took a lot of the labour force away from the more rural farms, leaving the very young, the old and the infirm to cultivate the land. Not surprisingly, agricultural production declined, and so did the export of cash crops. Eventually, the import of crops had to increase. With oil money, Nigeria started importing raw materials from other countries and, as a result, manufacturing became established. Many industries in Nigeria grew in food processing, vehicles, textiles, pharmaceuticals, paper and cement. By 1971 Nigeria had become a member of OPEC (Organization of the Petroleum Exporting Countries), which at that time was the world's seventh largest petroleum producer. A year after, the government took some steps towards trying to promote Nigerian enterprises. About 70% of the commercial firms in operation at that time were foreign-owned and the Nigerian government issued a decree to prevent foreigners from investing in specified enterprises, while it reserved participation in certain trades for Nigerians. The government also had to deal with the severe drought that affected the north between 1972 and 1974 (the most serious since that of 1913–1914). This caused famine in Nigeria and some Africans from neighbouring countries coming into Nigeria. Three years after that, in 1975, the government bought 60% of the equity in the marketing operations of the major oil companies in Nigeria. In 1974, oil prices rose dramatically worldwide, causing a sudden flood of wealth. The revenue that came into the country was intended for investment to diversify the economy but instead it led to inflation and a lot of unemployment. In 1975, oil production fell sharply because of the decrease in world demand, and the prices moved downward until later in the year when OPEC intervened to raise prices.

During the decline of oil prices, exports of traditional crops collapsed as a result of poor government policy and low prices on the world market. When Nigeria found itself importing a lot of food, various agricultural plans and policies were drawn up to try to produce cheaper food in sufficient quantities. Some of these were the Operation Feed the Nation (OFN) and Green Revolution (GR), and the Structural Adjustment Program (SAP). The techniques involved in these different programmes included large irrigation schemes, expansion of credit, using high-yielding seeds, dismantling the Commodity Boards, liberalising export trade, introducing incentives to boost farmers' outputs and assisting wheat-producing states. Also, other aspects of agriculture were started, including forestry and fisheries. By the early eighties the world recession sent oil prices plummeting again and this plunged Nigeria into a cycle of massive debt, soaring inflation, large-scale unemployment and widespread corruption. In 1986, market reforms, freeing exchange and interest rates, were introduced and this led to a sharp drop in the value of the Naira (the Nigerian unit of currency) while lending rates rose to more than 40%. Research showed that even if agriculture was able to go back to where it had been, the population growth was too huge for agriculture in the country to keep up with: the effect on Nigeria was so devastating that the country still imports food now. Matters became worse in 1996 when there were severe shortages of fertiliser, which further limited the agricultural production. Despite its resources, Nigeria is still considered a third-world country. The real standard of living has fallen sharply and this is attributed to the political instability, mismanagement and corruption, and the decline in oil prices. Development in terms of oil has been pretty rocky over the last few years. The execution of some environmentalists that protested led to many countries placing sanctions against Nigeria. Later some of those sanctions were removed but unfortunately oil troubles persisted. Environmental activists are still speaking up and protesting against oil companies in parts of Nigeria today because they believe it is ruining their environment. These protests and attacks have led to oil production losses and these troubles have slashed oil exports from Nigeria by more than one-fifth.

Population: Nigeria has one of the highest population densities in the world. At one time, it had the third highest population density and roughly one out of every four Africans was considered to be Nigerian. Population figures in Nigeria are usually estimated, and even these can differ. An estimate of 129 million is given to date.

Languages: There are several dialects spoken by different tribes but the main African languages spoken are Yoruba, Hausa and Ibo. Others are Edo, Efik and 'pidgin' or 'broken' English, a distorted version of English generally spoken by many. The general language spoken among the literates is English.

Culture: Nigerians celebrate many traditional festivals and countless numbers of cultures are adhered to. The Yorubas in Lagos celebrate the Eyo festival yearly. The Eyo is a masked man, who goes around the city on stilts with a lot of followers and lots of drumming and dancing. As the Eyo goes around town, he prays for people to live long to see him the next year. Also in Yoruba land is the Oro festival. The Oro is also a masked man but a very fearsome one. According to tradition, women are forbidden to see him. The Oro goes around in the night, naked with a group of men. If accidentally seen by a woman, she is compelled to make certain sacrifices to save her from losing her life. In Oshogbo in Oshun State, many traditional believers celebrate the Oshun festival yearly. These traditionalists pray to the goddess of Oshun river to give children to women who are barren and women who have been trying but unable to bear children. Lots of dancing and drumming accompany the rituals performed and women who believe in the power of this river are dipped into it with wrappers tied across their chest. Also in Ife in Oshun State is the Olojo festival. This is

african country guide

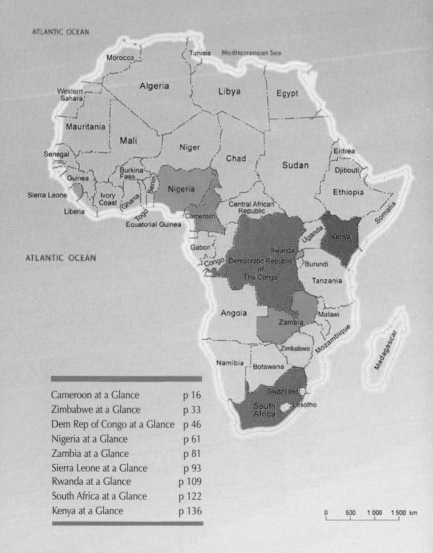

ATLANTIC OCEAN

Morocco

Tunisia   Mediterranean Sea

Algeria   Libya   Egypt

Western
Sahara

Mauritania

Mali

Niger

Senegal   Chad   Sudan   Eritrea

Burkina
Faso   Djibouti

Guinea

Sierra Leone   Nigeria   Ethiopia

Ivory
Coast   Ghana   Benin   Togo

Liberia   Cameroon   Central African
Republic   Somalia

Equatorial Guinea

Gabon   Uganda   Kenya

Congo   Rwanda

Democratic Republic
of
The Congo   Burundi

Tanzania

Angola   Malawi

Zambia

Zimbabwe   Mozambique

Namibia   Botswana   Madagascar

Swaziland

South
Africa   Lesotho

ATLANTIC OCEAN

0   500   1 000   1 500 km

Visit to Áras an Uachtarán
July 2005

Visit to Áras an Uachtarán
July 2005

Networking Waterford
October 2005

Networking Waterford
October 2005

Speaking Out
Intercultural Seminar June
2005 in Athlone

Traditional Attire
Nigeria

Speaking Out
Intercultural Seminar June
2005 in Athlone

Intercultural Seminar June
2005 in Athlone

FMG Focus Group
Athlone

FMG Focus Group
Athlone

FMG Focus Group
Athlone

FMG Focus Group
Athlone

FMG Focus Group
Athlone

FMG Focus Group
Athlone

Traditional Headgear
Nigeria

Traditional Headgear
Edo State, Nigeria

Traditional Attire
Romania

Traditional Headgear
Nigeria

Traditional Attire
Rwanda

Traditional Hair style
Kenya

Traditional Attire
Nigeria

Traditional Attire
Nigeria

AWN Executive Launch
with Tom Kitt
September 2003

Awarding of 'Trained to Represent' Certificates, September 2003

AWN at the
Mini Marathon
June 2003

celebrated yearly to mark the anniversary of the Oba's (king) reign. The Oba dons a special crown called 'Are' on this significant day. In the marriage culture all over Nigeria, polygamy is widely practised. A dowry is usually paid on the wife-to-be to the husband's family as a symbol of the bond between the two families. The bride price is more significant in the Ibo land where the price is very high. The Yorubas pay very little while some families in the Yoruba land don't accept it at all. Some Hausas pay the dowry when the bride is still a child. At this stage, the family of the child makes a vow to the man paying the bride price that she will not be given to anyone but him. (The man is usually old enough to be her father or grandfather) as soon as she is of age (usually in her early teenage years). Also in Ibo land is the New Yam Festival. This is celebrated every year when new yam tubers are harvested.

Ethnic groups: There are over 350 ethnic tribes in Nigeria, the three largest being Yoruba in the west, Ibo (also spelled Igbo) in the east, and the Hausa-Fulani in the north. Many of these ethnic groups have organisations worldwide.

Religion: To most Nigerians, religion and faith are important aspects of everyday life. It controls the laws, how they think and act, what they believe, what they value and much more. In Nigeria there are roughly 45% Christians, 45% Muslims and about 10% 'everything else', which includes traditional religions and beliefs.

Food: Just as Nigerian tribes are numerous, so are the different dishes that come with them. Nigeria is known for all kinds of interesting dishes made from traditional and local ingredients. In Lagos roadside stalls, called 'Buka', where the best cooked local cuisine is found, are very popular and they are the best chance of a good feed for many workers and students who hardly have time to cook because of the hustle and bustle of the city. Peppery stews are common in the southern states while menus of grains and beef are common in the north. Much of Nigerian food is grain-based. Tuwo, made from maize and corn rice or millet, is as popular as Efo (vegetable soup), Egusi soup (made with melon seeds) and Isi-ewu (goat-head pepper soup). There are also lots of snack foods, including yam chips (fried yam), meat pastries and fried plantain (dodo). Palm wine, a natural juice from palm trees, is a favourite drink all over Nigeria, especially in the south where the trees are grown.

Tourist attractions: Nigeria is blessed with many tourist attractions, some of which are eye catchers and very impressive. Nigeria, as a developing country realising the importance of tourism, has through successive governments given its development the pride of place it deserves. Nigeria can be described as a land of variety and contrast. It ranges from the thick mangrove swamps of the south to the sparse shrubs of the arid north; from the humid weather of the south to the semi-temperate climate of the Jos plateau on to the harmattan haze of the north. Thus, the weather, wildlife, waterfalls, historical relics and captivating beaches coupled with the warm-hearted and culturally active population make tourism in Nigeria full of interesting delights. Nigeria, therefore, is a fertile ground for both local and foreign tourists who want to visit her tourist attractions either for investment or to appreciate the extent to which nature has blessed the country. It is almost impossible to deny Nigeria its pride of place amongst the richly endowed potential tourist destinations of the world.

Lagos: Lagos is a sprawling, steamy, overpopulated city with bumper-to bumper traffic. It is a city where just about anything can and does happen. It offers a number of unique experiences, with more nightclubs and live music than just about any other west African city. On Lagos Island, the national museum Onikan is worth a visit for its impressive bronze sculptures and ivory carvings from Benin city and for its mask and terracotta antiquities from Jos city. Another noteworthy exhibition in the museum is the bullet-riddled car in which Muritala Mohammed, a former head of state, was assassinated. The Eyo Monument at Idumota, the National Theatre and the coconut beach of Badagry are also notable attractions.

Badagry: Badagry, the former home of the slave trade in Lagos, Nigeria, is one of the best and most interesting tourist attractions in the country. Slave-trading activities gained prominence there between the 16th and 18th centuries. At that time young men and women were forcibly sold into slavery and taken from the shores of Badagry and other towns, like Quidah in the republic of Benin in Kotonou and Goree Island in Senegal, to far-away places like America and the Caribbean Islands to work on plantations. These slaves were humiliated and dehumanised in these countries. The black race then were regarded as beasts of burden and subjected to various abuses. Freedom for the black race came later with the abolition of the slave trade. Badagry remains a point of remembrance for those dark days.

The chains that were used tie the legs of the slaves together in the 18th century and the iron rings used to clip their mouths are still kept in Badagry for tourists to see. Also in this town is the oldest and first store building erected in the whole of Africa. It was in this building that Bishop Ajayi Crowther translated the Holy Bible from English into Yoruba.

Bauchi State: The Yankari game reserve in Bauchi State is a bird-watching dream with over 600 species rooting around its interior. This is Nigeria's most popular holiday resort, which was declared open in December 1962. The Yankari game reserve covers an area of about 900 square kilometres. Varieties of wild animals, birds and reptiles abound. They include lions, giraffes, elephants, cheetahs, monkeys, wild hunting dogs, gazelles, Egyptian cobras, marabou stork, crocodiles, African pythons, water buck, cattle, fowl, glossy ibis, foxes, baboons, Senegal parrots, cuckoos and so on.

Plateau State: Jos offers a wide range of attractions, some of which are the Wildlife Park, Kurra Falls, Shere Hills, the Jos Museum and zoological gardens.

Abeokuta: The giant and mighty Olumo rocks in Abeokuta in Ogun State, with hidden caves underneath them, are also very interesting behold. A climb to the top of the rocks, with assistance from expert guides, gives a good view of part of the sprawling city. The rocks are synonymous with the name of Abeokuta town where they are situated. The cave around the rocks offered sanctuary to the founding fathers of the town during the days of inter-tribal wars. The Egba people who inhabited the area also worshipped these rocks in the belief that they derived their natural strength and protection from supreme beings. Guided tours are conducted for visitors by duty guides. Other attractions in Ogun state are the Ebute Oni tourist beach and the Bilikisu Sungbo Shrine.

Oshogbo: Oshogbo, the cradle of Yoruba arts, is in Oshun State. Here the Oshun festival takes place every last week in August. Dancing and sacrificial rites are performed in the Oshun river, whose goddess is believed to provide barren women with children. The Oshun river rises in the hill north of Ilesha and flows through the western part of the country into Lagos' lagoons. It is one of the several rivers which are said to have been formerly human (female) until some traumatic event frightened or angered them into changing to water. Oshun was one of the wives of Sango, god of thunder. The myth of her dramatic change into a river is not as important as the fact that, like her husband, she is also a deity. The annual traditional worship at the Oshun Shrine near the Oshun river has virtually turned into a religious-cum-tourist festival. People from various parts of Nigeria and countries beyond come to the Oshun festival. The Ohsun grove has several sculptures and is one of the main attractions. Oshogbo town itself is virtually an artist town. Other attractions there are the ancient city walls, the Erin Ijesha Falls, and the Ado Awaye suspended lake.

Cross River State: The Obudu Cattle Ranch in Ogoja in Cross River State, which offers a range of outdoor activities, was built in the 1950s by enterprising expatriate Scottish ranchers. The cool climate in the area makes it an attractive place for walking or hiking. The ranch is over 1,524 metres above sea level and has temperate weather conditions, which ensures green vegetation and grazing of cattle round the year. The ranch is a tourist delight as a result of its various attractions. There is a natural swimming pool, horse riding, a beautiful waterfall to behold, a gorilla camp, bird watching, sporting facilities and accommodation. Other attractions in Cross River are the Agbokim Falls, Kwa Falls, Boshi Game Reserve, Mary Slessor Cottage and the national museum. The Agbokim Falls are a short distance away from the Nigeria-Cameroon border. They are a very captivating sight. They lie less than 30 kilometres from Ikom and are highly recommended for picnics, as they are pleasantly surrounded by green vegetation. The Cross River National Park is about an hour's drive from Calabar and can also be linked through the Port Harcourt route. It is in the forest zone of south-east Nigeria. It has two sections, the southern urban division near Calabar and the northern Okwangwo near Obudu.

Kebbi State: Kebbi State is endowed with abundant tourism potential, because of its physical environment and people. There are historical relics, contemporary arts and crafts and cultural heritage in the form of festivals. The Argungun fishing festival dates to the 16th century. It has its origin in one of the local fishing festivals called Su.

But the little local event was given a wilder dimension in 1934 and has since then included traditional wrestling, boxing, archery, motor rallying and agricultural shows. The festival attracts visitors from other countries. Participants are mainly from Sokoto and neighbouring states and some are from Niger Republic. Fishing is done by traditional methods only. The fisherman with the biggest catch receives a prize.

CHAPTER FOUR

Nina
Nigeria

Nina watched with horror while an ear-splitting scream seized the air. The grip of five hefty men bit hard into Onome's skin, pinning her body to the ground. Beads of sweat laced her forehead as her body shook with pain. Agonising, excruciating pain shot through her. As she lay with her back on a hand-woven mat and her legs forced wide apart by these men, blood trickled freely down her thighs. A smile of satisfaction and relief lit Onome's mother's face. The next day, she would bask in the glory of being a proud mother. She would now be able to boast to the world that her daughter was free of promiscuity. Another man bent over Onome, using unsterilised sharp instruments to cut through the protective skin of her private parts. Slowly, she began to lose consciousness.

Carefully shielded behind a pole, Nina watched Onome go through the gruesome ordeal of female circumcision. As she watched, she prayed fervently for her not to die. She could almost hear her heart pounding heavily against her chest as she stood there, thinking of how she could help her friend. She kept wondering if this act really curtailed promiscuity or if was a question of morality or control over girls, or a form of torture. Onome almost lost her life. Nina blamed herself for not helping her friend. They were so young and helpless. She was scared of being chosen to be the next in line. She ran from behind the pole, drenched in sweat.

Female genital mutilation (FGM) - also known as female circumcision is one of the most widespread violations of the rights of African women in many African countries. Its exact historical origins are not known but it has been passed down through generations as an aspect of culture and of strongly held beliefs. Female circumcision is either performed on individuals, groups of sisters, close female relatives or neighbours. It is usually carried out as part of an initiation ceremony and is likely to be carried out on all the girls in the community who belong to a particular age group. The procedure may be carried out in the girl's home, in the home of her relative or neighbour, in a health centre or at a specially designated site, such as a particular tree or river, when associated with initiation. The person performing the mutilation may be an older woman, a traditional midwife or healer, a barber or a qualified midwife or doctor.

In most cases female genital mutilation is forcibly imposed on girls and young women by their family and community members. They are left with no other choice but to respond to the pressures of societal norms. The age at which circumcision is performed varies. It ranges from a few days old to adolescence and, occasionally, adulthood. It is considered a rite of passage from childhood to adulthood.

Girls undergoing the procedure have varying degrees of knowledge about what will happen to them. Sometimes a trained midwife will be available to give a local anaesthetic but, in some cultures, the girls are told to sit beforehand in cold water, to numb the area and reduce the likelihood of bleeding. More commonly, however, no steps are taken to reduce the pain. The girl is immobilised, held usually by older women or men who force her legs open.

Mutilation may be carried out using broken glass, a tin lid, scissors, a razor blade or some other sharp cutting instrument. In some cases after the act has been performed, thorns or stitches may be used to hold the two sides of the labia majora together, and the legs may be bound together for up to 40 days. Antiseptic powder may or may not be applied and in some cases pastes containing herbs, milk, eggs, ashes or dung, which are believed to facilitate healing, are applied. The girl may then be taken to a specially designated place to recover where, if the mutilation has been carried out as part of an initiation ceremony, traditional teaching is imparted. For those who are rich, the mutilation procedure may be performed by a qualified doctor in a hospital under local or general anaesthetic. Women and children who do not allow themselves to be laid open to these procedures are presumed to be shameful and abnormal in their societies, so in cases where FGM is an accepted and compulsory practice, women who refuse to undergo it may be considered to have transgressed social mores and be persecuted.

Many people fear that when a woman's clitoris is left at its natural shape and size she will have a higher libido and urge for sexual gratification. According to those who believe in it, if she does not get the gratification when she desires it, she will chase after it, which automatically makes her promiscuous. To control this desire, the act of circumcision, which involves trimming the clitoris to near non-existence, will curb a woman's sexual needs. With the medical revelation of the capability of the clitoris to aid fertilisation outside sexual pleasures, those who are circumcised will no doubt feel cheated out of a natural reproductive process. Circumcision is a practice in which girls and young women undergo physical cutting. It causes extraordinary pain and even after many years can lead to serious and permanent disability or death.

The protective skin is trimmed or cut off the vulva, leaving the more sensitive inner flesh exposed and liable to a high risk of infection. Over the years, the infection can spread through the womb, leaving permanent damage in most girls, who can no longer conceive. It is rare for women to survive mutilation without long- or short-term complications. The immediate ones include severe pain, shock, haemorrhage, acute urine retention and fractures. Later in life cysts and abscesses, scars, urinary incontinence, urinary tract infection, infertility, painful menstruation, sexual difficulties and many other complications develop. There have also been histories of psychological effects. Despite the lack of scientific evidence, personal accounts of mutilation reveal feelings of anxiety, terror, humiliation and betrayal, all of which would be likely to have long-term negative effects, but the most important psychological effect on a woman who has survived is the feeling that she is acceptable to her society, having upheld the traditions of her culture and made herself eligible for marriage, often the only role available to her. It is possible that a woman who did not undergo genital mutilation could suffer psychological problems as a result of rejection by the society.

Many years after that incident, Nina found herself fleeing her homeland to seek refuge in Ireland because the ordeal had affected her mentally and psychologically. The image she carried with her from Nigeria to Ireland is still very vivid in her mind and replays itself when stories of similar experiences are narrated to her. That was the first time she witnessed such an ordeal, though she had heard so much about it in the past. Her goal is to fight and stop such barbaric acts, which she regards as gender discrimination and an act of violence against women. Even as she narrates the story to me, her forehead is laced with sweat. Her scars grow deeper when Nina realises it is not likely her friend will ever conceive. She had learned later that Onome had been affected with a terrible infection that had eaten deep into her womb as a result of the unsterilised instruments used on her many years ago. Bitterness raged through Nina as she poured out her heart to me. Taking it all in, I sat down with my ears wide open, taking notes and digesting every word as it came out of her mouth.

For many months when Nina was still quite young in school, she pleaded to her aunt who housed her not to make her go through the inhuman process of female circumcision. Her aunt Comfort explained to her that it was necessary for every woman to be circumcised. She believed a stigma of shame would stain their family name and evil would follow them for the rest of their lives if she refused her daughter or any young girl under her care circumcision. She had repeatedly told Nina that any girl who died in the process of circumcision was a witch who deserved no pity. It was a life tradition handed down by their forefathers, and her family would not be an exception to the rule. Those who had refused their daughters' being circumcised were regarded as outcasts and labelled evil. They were usually sent out of the village and people were warned never to associate with them. Circumcision to Comfort was the best thing that could happen to a woman.

Nina had her primary school education in the western part of Nigeria and, later, finished it in the eastern region. After that she went to an all-girls secondary school, where she lived as a boarding student. School was fun. Nina was very pretty, and she knew it from the compliments she got from her friends and the comments passed by her mother's friends. She didn't hide her pride and her friends in school often bullied her. At that time, she believed they bothered her because she was quiet and very pretty. She believed there was something about her looks that disturbed her classmates, even though they were too young to understand such things.

Nina stayed in the boarding school for five years. There was lots of fun and parties for the girls, and every Saturday they organised a social gathering. There was also a performing cultural group. Nina was a very good dancer and this made her popular. One evening, a senior prefect who had admired Nina for a long time approached her and asked if she would be her school daughter. It was not uncommon for a senior student to have a junior student as her school daughter. (The term 'school daughter' is used for a junior student who was treated like a daughter by a senior student). Just like a real mother or guardian would do, the senior ones were meant to guide and protect the junior ones, paying particular attention to how they fared in school. Nina agreed. She liked 'prefect Agnes', as she was fondly called. Agnes came from a rich and well-cultured background and Nina's friend's envied her the more. From then on Nina got gifts, attention and special treatment from her school mother. On a typical day, students would get up early to clean their house. (Students were divided into different houses, which made up the boarding school). Nina escaped cleaning in the mornings because her school mother was one of the supervising prefects. She rarely allowed Nina to lift a finger. Nina was also a good handball player, and after she left secondary school, she kept up with the game, becoming an expert at it.

On one occasion Nina broke a school rule. Her father had dropped her back at school after spending a few days at home. Nina waved goodbye and walked into the school. As soon as her father's car disappeared, she looked around to see if anyone was watching. Satisfied the coast was clear, she sneaked out of the school to buy chocolates, which her father had banned her from eating. As she made her way out, her school principal spotted her from across the road. Nina tried to dodge her principal, who was almost knocked down by a motorbike as she made an attempt to cross the road to Nina. The principal was cross. She sent for Nina's father. In an attempt to play smart, Nina lied, saying that she had left the school to rescue her principal when she noticed a bike almost knocked her down. She twisted the story around, leaving the principal and her father puzzled.

Another interesting part of Nina's school life was her English class. Her English teacher was an American. The dream of every girl in Nina's class was to go to America and, because of this, Tony the American teacher meant everything to them. His accent especially fascinated and thrilled them and they gapped in awe every time he taught them. He was an idol and every student vied for his attention. The teacher gave them a surprise one day when he sent a latecomer out of the class. It was unusual. The class became unruly, making mocking comments. The girl he sent out was so ashamed of herself and felt so belittled that she decided to get even. As she made her way out of the class, she bent and picked up her books and, as she stood up, she swung around and hit the teacher in the face, sending his glasses flying. The whole class went wild with laughter. The class was later punished for this and Evelyn, the girl who caused it all, was suspended.

One day as Nina listened to the radio something caught her attention. A young girl's voice came on. 'I was genitally mutilated at the age of ten. I was told by my late grandmother that they were taking me down to the river to perform a certain ceremony, and afterwards I would be given a lot of food to eat. As an innocent child, I was led like a sheep to be slaughtered. Once I entered the secret bush, I was taken to a very dark room and undressed. I was blindfolded and stripped naked. I was then carried by two strong women to the site for the operation. I was forced to lie flat on my back by four strong women, two holding tight to each leg. Another woman sat on my chest to prevent my upper body from moving. A piece of cloth was forced in my mouth to stop me screaming. I was then shaved. When the operation began, I put up a big fight. The pain was terrible and unbearable. During this fight, I was badly cut and lost blood. All those who took part in the operation were half-drunk with alcohol. Others were dancing and singing and, worst of all, had stripped naked. I was genitally mutilated with a blunt penknife. After the operation, no one was allowed to aid me to walk. The stuff they put on my wound stank and was painful. These were terrible times for me. Each time I wanted to urinate, I was forced to stand upright. The urine would spread over the wound and would cause fresh pain all over again. Sometimes I had to force myself not to urinate for fear of the terrible pain. I was not given any anaesthetic in the operation to reduce my pain, nor any antibiotics to fight against infection. Afterwards, I haemorrhaged and became anaemic. This was attributed to witchcraft. I suffered for a long time from acute vaginal infections.'

Nina was scared. She had heard about girls being mutilated but didn't know what it really stood for. Nina was worried. She ran to her aunt. She wanted an explanation. The words of the young girl followed her every step. Her aunt dismissed her fear but had nothing to say. She assured Nina no such thing would happen to her, and that she would understand circumcision better as she grew up. Nothing was ever said about it again and Nina never thought about it until a very fearful incident that she would never forget happened.

It was in her last year in secondary school. It was the school inter-house sports day. Students would normally dress in sports wear. There were different kinds of competitions, involving different kinds of sports. It was a day everyone looked forward to every year. The marching parade was what Nina particularly liked because it afforded her the opportunity of showing off her well-cleaned and neatly ironed dress. A week before the sports day, Nina would soak her sports dress in a bucket of water and bleach for a whole day before washing it. Ironing the pleats of the dress was another thing she derived pleasure in doing. Her last year in school was the most special to her. She was determined to impress her friends. The day before the event she plaited her hair in a very special way and, on the day of the event, she wore a new dress she had bought with all her savings.

Halfway through the activities, Nina was told by one of her friends, Arinola, that her uncle wanted to see her. Nina was surprised. She wasn't expecting any of her uncles. Because she was sceptical and suspicious, she begged Arinola to follow her to see the man who was looking for her. Two hefty men stood at the gate of the school. Their faces looked strange to Nina, who stared at them, trying to figure out if she had seen any of them in her house before. One of them beckoned to her. She hesitated as she approached them. Standing far away from them, Nina asked what they wanted and who they were. One of them explained that the head of the village, a traditional chief, had asked them to bring her because of an important issue he had discussed with her aunt. She demanded to know what the issue was. The man explained that she was due for female circumcision, and that the necessary ritual and preparations were fixed for the next day. Nina's legs shook as the word sank in. She looked at the strange faces in shock. They approached her and, as they did, Nina held Arinola's hand and they began to walk backwards slowly and carefully. In the twinkle of an eye, one of the men grabbed Nina's hand and as he did she screamed. She struggled with him and her dress was ripped. Arinola ran as fast as she could, screaming for help. As soon as the men realised the noise had attracted some people, they bolted.

Nina never went back home to her aunt. Arinola took her home to her parents, who housed her until after she finished school. After they left from school, Nina left Arinola's family and relocated to Kaduna in the northern part of the country. She got a job as a ticketing officer. She did this for two years so she could save money for her education. She was admitted to read psychology at the Katsina Polytechnic. It was a new and exciting experience for her. Along the way, Nina lost concentration in school and was recommended for regular counselling because she couldn't make up her mind what she wanted to do. The idea was to help her recognise her potential and talents and start on a good foundation in life. She changed to studying insurance. The next four years were challenging and, after this, she graduated.

Nina got a job. Living was good and the prospect of a bright future was there. It did not take her long to meet the man of her dreams and, after a brief courtship, they were married in a colourful ceremony. Things went well for her and her husband for the first few years of the marriage. However, the situation changed when Nina's mother-in-law started despising her for not having any children. Her marriage began to shake. As the years went by, and she still didn't have a child, her mother-in-law did not hide her hatred towards her and also never relented in making her son Mike hate her. Everything Nina did was condemned and nothing looked right to Mike any more. He complained about her cooking, dressing, habits and anything he could pick on. The more they stayed together, the more he hated her and made her life miserable. In the middle of it all, Nina lost her mother in 1994. Though she had died far away in America, her loss left a big vacuum, which till today is still in Nina's heart. The situation was devastating as Nina was faced with a hostile husband, a wicked mother-in-law and the death of her mother. She bore the pain until the day her mother-in-law came home from a visit to her village with a young girl. Summoning Nina and Mike, she told them she had brought a new wife for her son to marry and if Nina had any objection to it she was free to find her way out. There ensued an argument between Mike and his mother. Nina kept mute, watching. The girl, Bose, was confused. She was too young to understand what was happening. Nina's mother-in-law explained further that the girl was a young virgin who would bear her as many grandchildren as she wanted. Mike refused bluntly and insisted his mother and the girl move out. His mother raved and ranted and swore that Nina would be the one to leave and not the girl.

A few weeks later, when things became unbearable for Nina, she moved out of the house, ending her marriage of six years. Not long after that she filed for a divorce and started a new life again, praying and hoping for the best in the future.

Her past traumas gradually began to fade from her mind. A few years after, she met someone else and, though Nina had made up her mind not to rush into anything, she found herself being married to Fredrick a couple of years after they met: she was pregnant. Her joy knew no bounds. She looked forward to raising her child. She was happy to be settled with a man who showered her with affection and devotion. They lived in one of the best bungalows in a village in Katsina in the northern part of Nigeria where Fredrick worked. They were happy. Their daughter arrived, and later a son.

Things went well for them for years. Then the economic crunch in the country started biting hard on the family. Inflation bit hard into the nation as oil prices went up, plunging Nigeria into a cycle of massive debt and large-scale unemployment. Political instability and mismanagement contributed to standards of living falling sharply.

At one point, Nina and Fredrick could no longer afford to eat three square meals a day. Some days, they only ate once; the food sometimes came from one of their neighbours. Fredrick lost his job. The economic constraints in the country had caused his company to fold up. The situation hit them really hard and Nina was left with the responsibility of taking care of the house and paying all the bills from the little she earned. Fredrick tried to get another job but all his efforts were in vain. Curiosity was aroused in him when he discovered that most of the people around him who were still surviving the crunch were Muslims. He was a devoted Christian of the Catholic faith and only had a few Muslim friends who were his neighbours. His parents had brought him up as a Catholic and all his life he had never practised any other religion. He found out that Muslims all over the country were being favoured in many ways. They were considered first when it came to getting government contracts and jobs. The president of the country was a Muslim and most of the influential people and top government dignitaries working in most states in the country were also Muslims. Katsina was also predominantly a Muslim state with just one-tenth of its inhabitants belonging to other religions. Fredrick decided to change his faith. He converted and started to practise the Islamic religion to the core. He believed he would make friends in high places, get a better job and contracts like other Muslims, and his financial situation would improve. He began to involve himself deeply with traditional Muslim practises and centred his life's entire plan on the religion. He abandoned his Christian friends for his Muslim counterparts and was happy to do anything they wanted in a bid to please them. It paid off, because things began to change for them again. Fredrick not only got a better job, he was also ranked high as one of the directors of the company that employed him. Nina's life changed again and, once more, they settled down to a better life with a promising future. But her dream was short lived.

Nina came back home from evening mass one day to meet a group of people in the house. Five men and a woman were engrossed in a discussion with her husband. As she walked into the house, they stopped talking, looked at each other and then gave her a long look. Nina stared at them, puzzled, but said nothing. Fredrick held her hands and explained to her that his Muslim friends had come to take her and their daughter away for circumcision. He explained that the woman in their midst was meant to perform the ritual while the men were meant to support her. Nina said nothing. She shuddered as memories of Onome's gruesome ordeal came flooding back to her. She looked at the men, again imagining them forcefully pinning her down for the woman to mutilate her. She knew them and had heard a lot about them. There was no home they visited without taking a woman or girl away for circumcision. No one had ever stopped them. It was the custom of the village.

Nina sat down, pretending to rest her feet. She showed no sign of objection or that she was scared, but she was. She couldn't understand Fredrick's attitude, but she said nothing.

As she sat thinking, her baby came to her rescue. He let out a sharp cry. Nina got up, excused herself to change the baby and went out of the room. As fast as she could she packed a few things for herself and her baby into a bag. She tried to think of the best way to go about it but time was too short. She took essentials and, with tears rolling down her cheeks, she opened the bedroom's back door. It led to the back of the house. She carefully shut the door and quietly made her way into her neighbour's garden. She ran as fast as she could, clutching her baby tightly to her chest and pulling her little girl's hand. A couple of times, her little girl, Lucy, stumbled and fell. Nina got her up and struggled on until she got to her sister's place. Her sister Ayaba hid and housed her while she made plans to move her to a safer place. Nina stayed with Ayaba until the day she got information that Fredrick had found out where she was and had vowed to send people to kidnap her. Not wasting a second, Ayaba took her away from her house to her friend's house. Nina left her daughter Lucy behind at her sister's. It was easier to cope with one child under such uncertain circumstances.

Nina stayed with her sister's friend Deola for a week until an arrangement was made for her to travel to Lagos. She stayed in hiding with her son for months. During these months, her mind was never at rest. She cried her eyes out every time she remembered her daughter and, though she blamed Fredrick for it all, she still missed the good times they had together. She believed he was being influenced and was unaware of the implications of what he was doing.

Ayaba slaved day and night to put money together for Nina. She approached a wealthy merchant from the northern part of Africa. The man was sympathetic. He lived in the Middle East with his family but promised to help Nina out of the country to a safe place. He got her an international passport and a ticket. Saying a tearful and brief goodbye to Ayaba and Lucy, Nina left her hiding place one evening to board a flight. Flagging down a cab to take her to the airport, the merchant handed over an address to her, bade her farewell and wished her luck in her new home.

Zambia at a Glance

History: Zambia's history goes back to the debut of Homo sapiens; it has evidence of human habitation going back 100,000 years. Beginning around 1000 AD, Swahili-Arab slave-traders gradually penetrated the region from their city-states on the eastern coast of Africa. Between the 14th and 16th centuries a Bantu-speaking group known as the Maravi migrated from present-day Congo and established kingdoms in eastern and south-eastern Zambia. In the 18th century, Portuguese explorers following the routes of Swahili-Arab slavers from the coast into the interior became the first known European visitors. After the Zulu nation to the south began scattering its neighbours, victims of the Defiance (forced migration) began arriving in Zambia in the early 19th century. The celebrated British explorer David Livingstone travelled up the Zambezi in the 1850s, searching for a route into the interior of southern Africa, hoping to introduce Christianity and European civilisation to combat the horrors of the slave trade. Livingstone's efforts attracted missionaries, who in turn brought hunters and prospectors in their wake. In the 1890s much of Zambia came under the control of the British South Africa Company (BSAC), which sought to prevent further Portuguese expansion in the area. The territory of Northern Rhodesia was administered by the South Africa Company from 1891 until it was taken over by the UK in 1923. The colony was put under direct British control in 1924 and in 1936 Lusaka became the capital. During the 1920s and 1930s, advances in mining spurred development and immigration. The head of state in the fifties founded the United National Independence Party (UNIP), advocating the end of British rule. That rule ended in 1963, when the federation dissolved and Northern Rhodesia took the name Zambia, after the Zambezi River. Independence came too late to halt the haemorrhaging of money occurring under British rule. Following independence, the head of state led Zambia for 27 years, a feat he accomplished by declaring the UNIP the only legal party and himself the sole presidential candidate. Calling his mix of Marxism and traditional African values 'humanism', he rapidly bankrupted the country with a bloated civil service and a nationalisation scheme wracked by corruption and mismanagement. Disastrous politics in the

1970s and 1980s led to poverty and the virtual breakdown of the country. Falling copper prices and rising fuel prices accelerated the slide and by the end of the 1970s Zambia became one of the poorest countries in the world. This touched off nationwide riots which killed thousands and a further round of price hikes in the early 1990s led to more rioting but this time Zambians demanded a multiparty democracy. Full elections in 1991 brought an end to one-party rule, but the subsequent vote in 1996 saw blatant harassment of opposition parties. The new head of state also set about reforming the civil service and reprivatising or closing failed government enterprises. He effectively eliminated all serious opposition and triumphed easily. Two independent election monitors who dared to suggest that the election was neither free nor fair were arrested. The election in 2001 was marked by administrative problems, with two parties filing legal petitions challenging the results. But by the end of the nineties the fortunes of Zambia had changed, as a massive shift on the political scene lead to economic reforms and other improvements. Despite the political chaos, the 2001 election, however flawed, returned one of the most broadly based democratic parliaments the country had seen, putting an end to the rubber-stamp, one-party system that had ruled the country since independence. Land-locked Zambia is one of Africa's most eccentric legacies of colonialism and for many years it has been the Cinderella of Africa, often overlooked by tourists and forgotten by the rest of the world.

Economy: Despite progress in privatisation and budgetary reform, Zambia's economy is still shaky. In the 1980s and 1990s, declining copper prices and a prolonged drought hurt the economy. Privatisation of government-owned copper mines relieved the government from covering mammoth losses generated by the industry and greatly improved the chances for copper mining to return to profitability and spur economic growth. However, low mineral prices slowed the benefits from privatising the mines and reduced incentives for further private investment in the sector. In late 2000, Zambia was determined to be eligible for debt relief under the Heavily Indebted Poor Countries (HIPC) initiative. Unemployment rates are high and inflation remains close to 20%. The major industries in Zambia are copper mining and processing, construction, foodstuffs, beverages, chemicals, textiles and fertiliser.

Population: It is estimated that Zambia has a population of about 10 million with the capital city Lusaka having as much as 1.5 million.

Languages: English and over 70 indigenous languages are spoken in Zambia. English is the national language and it is widely spoken, even in remote areas.

Culture: The Zambian people celebrate many traditional festivals. The best-known festival is the Kuomboka, held near the town of Mongu in western Zambia towards the end of the rainy season in late March or early April. During the festival the Lozi chief (village chief) and his family are paddled in massive war canoes across the Zambezi river floodplains, from their palace at Lealui to Limulunga. Also in early March anglers set their poles for the Zambia National Fishing Competition held on Lake Tanganyika. In late February, the N'Cwala festival is held at Mutenguleni, during which the chief of the Ngoni people samples the year's first fresh produce and commemorates the Ngoni's entrance into Zambia in 1835. The event is marked by feasts, music and some of the best dancing in the country.

Ethnic groups: There are about 35 different ethnic groups or tribes in Zambia, all with their own languages. The main groups and languages include Bemba in the north and centre, Tonga in the south, Nyanja in the east and Lozi in the west. The smaller groups include Ngoni, Lunda, Kaonde, Luvale, Asian (1%) and European (1%).

Religion: About two-thirds of the population are Christians though many combine that with traditional animist beliefs. It is estimated that the Christians make up 50–75%, the indigenous beliefs 50–75% and the remaining follow both.

Food: The staple dish in Zambia is a stiff porridge called Nshima. This is commonly made from maize or sometimes sorghum. It's typically served in a communal dish and eaten with the right hand, rolling the nshima into a ball and dipping it into a sauce of meat or vegetables. In areas along rivers and lakeshores, fish are also eaten. Popular freshwater types of fish include bream, lake salmon and Nile perch.

Tourist attractions: Zambia has many excellent safari opportunities, mainly in its great national parks, with endless opportunities for photos as well as a mind-boggling array of adventurous activities to choose from. Lusaka, the capital of Zambia, is a sprawling, swollen city surprisingly rich in galleries featuring local artists. Among the best are the Henry Tayali Visual Arts Gallery, the Mpala Gallery and the sculpture garden at the Garden House Hotel. For wildlife fans, the excellent national parks are teeming with birds and animals and boast some of the finest safari camps and lodges in the whole of southern Africa. All the major national parks (South Luangwa, Lower Zambezi and Kafue) are excellent for bird watching. Another good bird-watching spot is Lake Itezhi-Tezhi, where herons, spoonbills and many other water birds roost.

On top of this, the country shares (with Zimbabwe) the Victoria Falls and the Zambezi river – two of the region's major tourist highlights. The Zambezi river offers outstanding canoeing and white-water rafting, while the bridge and gorge downstream of Victoria Falls offers bungee jumping, abseiling, rock climbing and hiking. Also famous in Zambia are walking safaris, where you leave behind all modern trappings and follow an experienced ranger. Nothing beats being on foot in the African bush for sharpening the senses and heightening the wilderness experience! An evening boat tour with a few drinks, known locally as a 'booze cruise', is also very popular. The Kafue National Park is Zambia's largest home to grassland plains stretching for hundreds of kilometres. It is prime safari territory with lions, leopards, elephants, rhinos, antelopes, zebras and even ultra-rare yellow-backed duikers to prove it. Without a doubt, in Zambia you come pretty close to finding the 'real' Africa.

CHAPTER FIVE

Chileshe
Zambia

Chileshe tapped her hand on the table in irritation. A dozen and one things raced through her head. She eyed the books in front of her. The last thing on her mind was reading. Being saddled with the responsibility of taking care of her brother and younger sisters, especially the one that was ill, made her lose concentration. The nagging thought of the burden in front of her weighed her down but she was determined to go the extra mile. She paced up and down, then sat and bowed her head in prayer. Tears rolled down her cheeks as she lifted up her voice in a plea to the Most High. She remembered her late parents and kept asking why they had to go like that. In the room next to hers, a few of her sisters stared at each other, as if the solution to their problems lay on their foreheads. The others had gone out to hawk food in the streets. They all in the past been exposed to risks and had faced the humiliation of being attacked in the dark. Sometimes they lost all they had to hoodlums and, other times, they ended up with cuts and bruises. A few times, they had narrowly escaped hit-and-run drivers. Despite all this, they carried on, determined not to rest until they found a solution to their problems.

In the small two-bedroom bungalow where Chileshe, her six sisters and brother were cramped, you could feel the presence of poverty. Though the house looked simple and neat, everything else spelt poverty. The food shelves were empty and the bedrooms had mattresses placed on hand-woven mats on the floor. The gasoline stove for cooking was so old and rusty its fragile weight could hardly carry a large pot. The air in the neighbourhood was foul and harsh but, surprisingly, they carried on their daily chores in contentment and never lost hope for a better life. The extent of poverty they experienced fired Chileshe's determination to equip herself and her siblings with a good education, which she still believes is the most potent weapon against poverty.

During her story, Chileshe occasionally stopped and shook her head, as if telling me that I could never imagine how bad it had been for them. Each time I tried to reassure her, a faint smile lit her face. Before she began the story of her life, Chileshe expressed her gratitude and complimented AkiDwa for taking the initiative to ask African women in Ireland to air their views. Her hope is that the organisation continues to support women in various circumstances, addressing their needs and issues seriously and, above all, empowering them to be valuable members of society so they don't feel left out as foreigners. She was concerned about the young women out there in dire circumstances whose voices cannot be heard. As an African woman in a foreign country, she knows this could make it difficult to have access to freedom of expression. Her words came pouring out with my first question and I began to write as the picture of the story of Chileshe's life unfolded itself to me.

Chileshe had lost her parents when she was in college doing a course in education. Her mother had died of severe malaria and two years after that her father had died of depression; shortly after he lost his wife, he had lost his job as well. The only hope Chileshe and her siblings had left had been in him. No matter how hard they had tried to comfort him, the more withdrawn he became. One day he returned home and fell ill of a strange ailment. He was taken to the hospital but died later, leaving Chileshe with the burden of taking care of her six younger sisters and a brother. Chileshe's father had been an engineer while her mother traded in foodstuffs. They had been very comfortable.

Chileshe began to face the difficulties of coping with life without help. She was left with all the responsibilities of her parents.

Her parents had taught them to be independent. Chileshe had learnt to do a lot of things on her own.

They lived in the capital city and her school was close to home. This allowed her to enjoy all the privileges her mother gave her, unlike other children who had to walk long distances to get to school. Most of the other young girls eventually left school and remained in the fields to carry on with domestic duties while the boys who could endure the long-distance walk to school continued with their education.

Usually, Chileshe and her sisters were up by 6.00 a.m. so they could make classes, which started at 6.45 a.m. By 10.00 a.m. school was finished and they would be back at home with their parents.

Chileshe never liked the inequalities she experienced in her primary school. Academically the primary curriculum did not promote inclusion of all children but rather it encouraged streaming through ability grouping. This had adverse effects on the pupils. Pupils were divided into three groups in class. One group consisted of those who were good in class, the second those who were not so good academically and the third those who performed poorly in class. But despite these exclusive practices Chileshe's primary education had less competition among pupils than her secondary education.

Generally school was fun and this made Chileshe look forward to her secondary-school experience. There was a rigid curriculum as well. Students were put in classes they didn't like by teachers who believed they would excel in these classes. Chileshe was placed in a science class because she passed her science subjects, and though she tried to make the teachers realise she wasn't good very at science, her efforts fell on deaf ears. Many students were forced to take subjects they did not like. Boys were offered more places and chances to access education than girls and that resulted in a lot of women not being educated enough to hold high positions after school. Most girls attained their highest qualification at primary level and over 50% of the population of girls were dropouts. Things got better in Zambia as women woke up from their slumber and fought for equal rights. To educate more girls, the curriculum and examinations in schools were modified so that more girls could attend schools and have access to third-level education. Many years after, the education system in Zambia changed as educationists began to move to a new thinking, implementing the kind of education and curriculum that included all children, especially the female child.

Though Chileshe hated the idea, she was forced to leave her parents when she was accepted into a secondary school. There were not too many secondary schools then and in those days; girls who got admission into any of the good ones were considered lucky.

She had to go and live with her paternal grandmother, whose house was closer to her school. The experience for her was an unpleasant one and she believed she would have done better academically if she had continued to live with her parents. For no reason she could think of, her grandmother, who was considered a

87

very wealthy woman, did not show her any love or affection. She even made Chileshe's situation worse by ignoring her needs. She was very strict and treated Chileshe like a stranger.

As Chileshe grew up she found herself having to practically beg her grandmother for everything she needed. Many times she wondered to herself if the woman was really her father's mother or if she had stolen him at birth. They were different from each other, miles apart in nature and, no matter how Chileshe tried, her grandmother just couldn't stand Chileshe's ways. She hated living with her but she had no choice.

Chileshe's most memorable moments at secondary school were the extracurricular activities she enjoyed after school hours. She was particularly interested in drama and games. At that time anyone who came top in five competitions in a row was considered a hero. Having a flair for competing, Chileshe participated in most of them.

When Chileshe left secondary school she went on to teacher-training college. But in her second year her parents died and she was left to take care of her siblings alone. Then one of her sisters, Pat, became very ill. She had been born with epilepsy and had struggled with it for many years. Epilepsy is a neurological condition. When an epileptic person's usual brain activity is suddenly disturbed a seizure can occur. Pat's condition became critical and Chileshe knew that if she did not make arrangements for her to be taken to a hospital she would die.

Chileshe had left Pat with her maternal grandmother, who was poor and struggling to make ends meet in their village. There were no hospitals in the village, only small clinics. Several times Chileshe had tried to get Pat into a hospital in the city, but she could not afford to pay the hospital bills. The situation for her was tight. She had little or nothing to feed herself and her siblings. Many times Chileshe tearfully approached her paternal grandmother for help. Each time her grandmother not only refused to help, but sent her away with a wave of her hand, as if the sight of her alone irritated her.

Not knowing what else to do, Chileshe ran to one of her uncles. In tears, she begged him for help. At first he also refused, but eventually he agreed to house the sick girl for just two days, time for Chileshe to find an alternative solution. Chileshe left Pat with him, with the promise that they would not stay an hour longer than he wanted.

She combed the whole city, trying to find a Good Samaritan who could help her sister. Two days later, when nothing was forthcoming, she approached an orphanage where she believed her sister would get adequate care and help and then transferred Pat to the orphanage. Chileshe worked very hard and sent money regularly for Pat's upkeep. Her other siblings were still in school.

Things went on well for a few months but as soon as Chileshe's uncle felt she was earning enough money to take care of herself he sent her packing from the house. Chileshe went looking for assistance. For a very long time no help came their way. She approached her employers. Her joy knew no bounds when the company allocated her a small two-bedroom bungalow. She was happy she could live as a family with her siblings. Even though it was tight, they moved in and lived together. They began to manage. Many times the seven of them shared what was ideally meant for two people. Constant hunger became a part of their lifestyle and many times they thought they were going to die, one after the other, of starvation or ill health. Sometimes they were so depressed they would have gladly welcomed death. They prayed to die in peace, rather than live in hopelessness. But hard as it was, they staggered on.

Getting medical care was like looking for water in a stone. There were too many things to be taken care of. They barely had clothes, shoes and food and for years their clothes and shoes were tattered and worn with age. Experience taught them to share with love. They shared the little they had as well as their joys and pains. Going through the trauma of poverty and being orphans at such a tender age taught them so many lessons about life. Education to them was the key to success, an instrument to quality of life, no matter how little the success was. It was this point of view that made Chileshe's interest in studying further and perhaps going abroad a priority to her.

After her teacher training, Chileshe took up a teaching job. After teaching for two years, Chileshe discovered that she couldn't cope with earning so little with so many responsibilities, so she decided to study further so she could get a higher position and better prospects at work. She went into Special Needs education and trained for a year, in 1998. She had to cope with paying her fees in school, as well taking care of herself and her sisters. Things became increasingly tight for her. She made an appeal to the college concerning her fees. Her plight was considered and a special arrangement was made for her to pay her school fees in installments. Her father's family, who were very wealthy, gave her very little support, despite knowing what she was facing.

After a year, she got a certificate and, knowing it was not enough, she went on to do a diploma for another two years.

Chileshe began to apply for scholarships to study abroad and, just before she graduated from college, she got a six-month scholarship to study in Norway. Though orphaned and left with such a great responsibility, she feels fortunate to have reached her level of education and most of all to have had the opportunity to study abroad. The seven of them were all in school, struggling with the challenges of life, when Chileshe got the schorlaship. Though the scholarship was for the same programme she had almost completed in two years, she felt it was a good opportunity she could not afford to miss. Chileshe withdrew from college and went to Norway. The trip to Norway started a turning point in her life. It opened doors and everything about her life began to take a positive turn.

She returned home at the end of her programme and was sad to see that life was still the way she had left it. But this did not discourage her. It was much easier for her to get a job because of the edge she had over many others. She not only had new skills and knowledge, she had studied abroad. The pay was not only better: the prospects were very good.

After working for some time Chileshe began to feel the pinch again. Feeding and educating her siblings, who were now teenagers, became increasingly difficult. She began to make more efforts to go higher in her education. She kept on applying for scholarships in different schools, through the Internet. There were so many refusals but the urge to survive kept pushing her. Any time she met with an obstacle, she lifted her hands in prayers. The search went on until she came home one day and found a message on her phone; she was to contact the Irish Embassy in Zambia concerning a scholarship she had been offered by University College Dublin (UCD) for a Higher Diploma in remedial and special education. The next week was a week of joy and celebrations for her and her siblings. Once more they saw a light at the end of the tunnel.

Every time Chileshe looked back, memories of the days when they got up, not knowing where the next penny or meal would come from, always came back to her. Today, she is proud of herself for surviving the obstacles she had to face as a young girl and for being able to successfully manage to educate her siblings. The past helped in planning for the future, made her strong and taught her to stand on her feet rather than be dependent on people. Glad that she was able to teach her sisters and brother to be brave and independent, her experiences had built a solid foundation, which she believes helped her to think big when she was faced with seemingly insurmountable problems. By the time she was through with the hard times she had a clearer picture and better understanding of why most young girls in Zambia who are faced with hard lives and bitter experiences end up in the streets as prostitutes. Seeing many young girls becoming victims of unwanted pregnancies, early marriages, illnesses, poverty and no education is of great concern to her. It is a situation she believes should be seriously addressed to save lives. In addition to the factors that make young women end up in the streets, there are also economic reasons that make them migrate to other countries in search of a better living and quality of life. Most of these women flee their homeland because they are faced with hunger, slave labour and destitution. Their living conditions are inhuman and miserable. Those who are educated but deprived of the basic amenities end up being a bit successful but poor. The ones who have no opportunity of going to school end up in prostitution or as victims of abuse. The economic situation in Zambia, however, does not permit a lot of young children to have the opportunity of going to school because many schools are for the rich and the comfortable. For all the years that Chileshe and her siblings fought hunger, poverty and illnesses, they fought the temptation of being pushed by their situation to end up in prostitution or another form of abuse.

Chileshe came to Ireland in 2000 under the Ireland Aid Scholarship, to study at University College Dublin (UCD) for 12 months. She encountered a lot of challenges, even though Ireland was not the first foreign country she had visited. Her experiences in the past were totally different from what she met in Ireland. She was faced with trying to adapt to the environmental factors and the culture. She admits to benefiting a lot in terms of academic enrichment. She has also experienced racism, which she'd never encountered elsewhere. This made her feel she had limited freedom and that her life generally would be better at home in Zambia if she had the means for survival. However, when Chileshe graduated from UCD, she was offered an award because of her exemplary performance to continue her programme. She had applied for her masters in Trinity College but though she was offered a place she did not have the funds to pay her fees and unfortunately couldn't get a scholarship.

She was forced to go back home to Zambia to work. She sought assistance from friends and colleagues. Even getting a scholarship in her own country seemed impossible and, after three months, when she realised she couldn't cope with the job she had, she returned to Ireland and continued with her search for funds. She managed to get sponsors for her tuition and was faced with providing her own living expenses through part-time jobs. Chileshe worked in her spare time to keep herself and her siblings.

Chileshe's living and studying in Ireland, besides other experiences, have been a blessing to her. She considers her university experience as being the greatest so far. Her hope is that, after her programme, things will change drastically for her and her siblings back home. She is happy that whatever little earnings she made have helped her family to have access to third-level education, which is extremely expensive in her country.

Having qualifications from Ireland gives her hopes for a better job and future back home. It is a challenge she is ready to face as a woman because, according to her, women all over the world have suffered marginalisation for too long.

Sierra Leone at a Glance

History: Over six centuries ago some tribes settled in the virgin forest protected by the sea on one side and the mountains on the other. In 1495, on the site of what is now Freetown, the Portuguese set up a trading post for gold, spices, ivory and slaves. European contacts with Sierra Leone were among the first in West Africa, and Sierra Leone was one of the first West African British colonies. Foreign settlement did not occur until 1787, when the British prepared a refuge within the British Empire for freed slaves. That year, the site of Freetown received 400 freedmen from Great Britain. Disease and hostility from the indigenous people nearly eliminated the first group of returnees. These returned Africans, or Creoles as they came to be called, were from all areas of Africa. Cut off from their homes and traditions by the experience of slavery, they assimilated British styles of life and built a flourishing trade on the West African coast. In the early 19th century, Freetown served as the residence of the British governor, who also ruled the Gold Coast (now Ghana) and the Gambia settlements. Sierra Leone served as the educational centre of British West Africa as well. The extraction of minerals began a few years after the First World War. In 1926 16,000 people were employed in the mining industry. The workers were ill paid and often badly treated. During the Second World War Freetown was an important Allied base. Seven thousand Sierra Leoneans volunteered for service and fought alongside the British. The indigenous people mounted several unsuccessful revolts against British rule and Creole domination. Most of the 20th century history of the colony was peaceful, however, and independence was achieved without violence. Independence came in April 1961 and Sierra Leone opted for a parliamentary system within the British Commonwealth. Sir Milton's Sierra Leone Peoples Party (SLPP) led the country to independence and the first general election under universal adult franchise was held in May 1962. Upon Sir Milton's death in 1964, his half-brother, Sir Albert Margai, succeeded him as Prime Minister. Sir Albert attempted to establish a one-party political system but met fierce resistance from the opposition All Peoples Congress (APC). In closely contested elections in March 1967, the APC won a majority of the parliamentary seats. The governor general (representing the British monarch) declared Siaka Stevens (APC leader and Mayor of Freetown) the new Prime Minister but within a few hours Stevens and Margai were placed under house arrest by Brigadier David Lansana, the Commander of the Republic of Sierra Leone Military Forces (RSLMF). He did this on the grounds that the determination of office should await the election of tribal representatives to the house. A group of senior military officers overrode this action by seizing control of the government on 23 March, arresting Brigadier Lansana and suspending the constitution. The group called itself the National Reformation Council (NRC), with Brigadier A.T. Juxon-Smith as its chairman. The NRC in turn was overthrown in April 1968 by a 'sergeants' revolt' from the Anti-Corruption Revolutionary Movement. NRC members were imprisoned and other army and police officers deposed. Stevens at last assumed the office of Prime Minister under the restored constitution. The return to civilian rule led to by-elections beginning in the fall of 1978 and the appointment of an all-APC cabinet. Tranquillity was not completely restored. In 1970, a state of emergency was declared after provincial disturbances, and in March 1971 and July 1974, alleged military coup plots were uncovered by the government. In 1971 Sierra Leone became a republic, with Stevens as president for a five-year term. He was re- elected by parliament in 1976. Siaka P. Stevens, who had been head of state of Sierra Leone for 18 years, retired from that position in November 1985, although he continued his role as chairman of the ruling APC party. In August 1985, the APC named military commander Joseph Saidu Momoh as the party candidate to succeed Stevens; he was Stevens' own choice. Momoh was elected president in a one-party referendum on October 1, 1985.

Sierra Leone has seen serious and grotesque human rights violations since 1991, when civil war erupted. The rebel war in the eastern part of the county posed an increasing burden on the country and, on 29 April 1992, a group of young officers launched a military coup which sent Momoh into exile in Guinea and established the NRC as the ruling authority in Sierra Leone under Captain Valentine Strasser. In 1996 Strasser was replaced by his former associate, Brigadier-General Julius Bio. Two months later, Bio handed over to an elected civilian government headed by Alhaji Tejan Kabbah. Sierra Leone's coup, the third in just over five years, threw the country into turmoil, abruptly ending Sierra Leone's hopes of reaching a lasting settlement to the violence that had devastated the country since 1991. The Economic Community of West African States (ECOWAS) imposed sanctions against the new regime but the military junta retaliated by hiring foreign shipping companies to import food and fuel. The blockade pushed Sierra Leone's already fragile economy to a state of near collapse and the price of rice, the country's staple food, more than trebled, bringing even more hardship. Fuel shortages meant no public transport and most available electricity was reserved for military and government facilities and hospitals. Many schools, offices and factories remained closed for a number of months after the coup as part of a civil disobedience campaign and there was a crippling shortage of cash following the damage and closure of the central bank during the coup. More than 300,000 people fled the country. Despite recent positive developments, Sierra Leone remains highly unstable. Diamond-rich Sierra Leone is one of the world's most impoverished countries but rampant corruption and ten years of bloody civil war has left the nation in tatters. Although the war was declared over in January 2002, the peace is still fragile. It is indeed ironic that Sierra Leone is one of the poorest countries in the world while it has a rich set of natural resources and minerals, including diamonds, which have caused other countries and corporations to fight over them.

Economy: Sierra Leone's economy is predominantly agricultural with most of its workers engaged in subsistence farming. The principal food crops are rice, cassava, corn, millet and peanuts. The leading cash crops, most of which are exported, are palm kernels, palm oil, cocoa and coffee. Poultry, cattle, sheep and goats are raised and the fishing industry is also important. The country has an important mining industry, which is largely controlled by foreign companies. The main minerals extracted are diamonds (the country's major source of hard currency), iron ore, gold, bauxite and rutile. However, the mining industry, like other areas of the economy, has been severely affected by civil strife. The cost of Sierra Leone's imports is higher than its earnings from exports. The principal imports are machinery, manufactured consumer goods, foodstuffs, transportation equipment and fuels and the chief exports are diamonds and other minerals, cacao, coffee and fish. Diamond smuggling has been a problem since the 1960s, and during the civil war much of the diamond-mining area fell into the hands of rebel groups. Serious social disorders continue to hamper economic development following an 11-year civil war and this has made the country an extremely poor African nation with tremendous inequality in income distribution. The fate of its economy now depends upon the maintenance of domestic peace and the continued receipt of substantial aid from abroad, which is essential to offset the severe trade imbalance and to supplement government revenues. Sierra Leone's leading trade partners are the European Union countries, the United States and Côte d'Ivoire.

Population: The population of Sierra Leone is estimated to be 4.4 million.

Languages: The languages spoken in Sierra Leone are English (official and its regular use is limited to a literate minority), Mende (the principal vernacular in the south), Temne (principal vernacular in the north) and Krio (English-based Creole, spoken by the descendants of freed Jamaican slaves who were settled in the Freetown area, a lingua franca and a first language for 10% of the population but understood by about 95%).

Culture: The most outstanding feature of Sierra Leone's cultural life is its dancing. The different communities of the nation have their own styles of costumes and dance. The carving of various wooden masks in human and animal figures for the dances is especially advanced in the southern region. The 'Sande Mask', worn on the head of the chief dancer attending the reappearance of the female initiates from their period of seclusion, is perhaps the most well known carved figure in Sierra Leone art. It is a symmetrically stylised black head of an African woman with an elaborate plaited pyramidal coiffure adorned with various figures and with a facial expression of grave dignity and beauty. Ivory figures are characteristic of the Sherbro, Bullon and Temme peoples of the coastal and northern regions. There are also steatite human figures, when distorted called 'nomoli' and when in wooden form called 'Pomtan' (plural for 'Pombo)', which before the 16th century were used for ancestor worship or fertility rites. At present they are used for ceremonies to ensure abundance of crops. The national museum tells the story of the history and culture of the country (particularly the influence of the formidable Mandinka warrior kings).

Amongst the most interesting exhibits in the museum is a copy of the De Ruyter stone, which, in 1948, was proclaimed one of Freetown's oldest monuments. In Freetown is a giant cotton tree. The story goes that the tree started life as a young sapling when settlers came to Freetown in 1787. It is buried six inches under the ground, just above the high water level, at Jimmy market place and is inscribed with the names of famous sailors. It has been uncovered and buried many times to protect it from vandalism.

Ethnic groups: There are 20 native African tribes, which make up 90% of the population (Temne 30%, Mende 30%, other 30%). Creoles (Krio) make up 10% (descendants of freed Jamaican slaves who were settled in the Freetown area in the late 18th century). There are also refugees from Liberia's recent civil war and small numbers of Europeans, Lebanese, Pakistanis and Indians.

Religion: Islam 60%, traditional beliefs 30% and Christianity 10%.

Food: Sierra Leone shares the cuisine of much of western Africa, which includes cassava, yams, plantains, bananas, red palm oil, peanuts and other fruits and vegetables. Fish is an important protein food in coastal areas and the Mende people in southeast Sierra Leone eat rice as their main staple food. Some Sierra Leoneans say that they do not consider themselves to have eaten if they haven't had rice. This love persists through the ages with the African American descendants of the enslaved people brought from Sierra Leone to America, the Gullah and the Gechee, being known among other things for their love of rice. Other favourites of the Sierra Leoneans are fried plantains and tapioca pudding. Tapioca comes from the processed root of the cassava. Another main meal of most Sierra Leoneans is 'plasas', a vegetable dish. The vegetable normally takes the form of a leaf, as in bitter leaves, cassava leaves (the leaf of the cassava plant) or potato leaves (the leaf of the sweet potato plant). Plasas is normally purchased from the market in bundles and is usually prepared with palm oil (oil from the palm kernel of the palm tree) but can also be prepared with vegetable oil. Plasas may also be prepared with neither palm oil nor vegetable oil and when prepared this way it is referred to as a 'whait (white) soup'. Groundnut paste may be added to the soup to make it tastier.

Tourist Attraction: All the natural resources on which to build a healthy tourism business are available in Sierra Leone. There's a warm tropical climate and smiling people who are rich in culture and waiting to welcome the world back to Sierra Leone. Miles of palm-fringed sandy beaches kissed by the sun all year round, green mountains with lush vegetation, African wildlife, seafood restaurants with fish freshly pulled from the ocean, a kaleidoscope of flora and fauna, colour and crafts and many more are all to be found in this country. There is also a display of diamonds, a major industry in Sierra Leone. The display shows how diamonds are transformed from rough stones to cut and finished gems. There are many masks and statues of significance in the country. A woodcraftsman is always available to demonstrate how the exotic African masks and statues are carved. Another attraction is the cloth weaver, who is also ready to show tourists how clothes are woven.

CHAPTER SIX

Iye Jillo
Sierra Leone

Iye Jillo walked towards the bus stop at Dublin Airport dragging her feet and luggage behind her. She queued for a bus to take her to the city centre. She tried to summon up the courage to ask questions, but she couldn't. She looked around her. The trees, shrubs and the road signs seemed to confirm to her that a new life awaited her. The journey that day had been hectic and tiring. It had not been a properly planned one, considering Iye was a prim and proper person who loved to do things in an orderly manner. Nothing had been planned, neither the trip nor what led to it. Disasters, accidents and wars are never planned.

For weeks that had run into months, Iye Jillo had tried to put her past behind her but like an incessant pang of hunger the thoughts kept nagging her. Iye still can't believe she had narrowly escaped being killed just over a month before her trip.

A tap on Iye's shoulder startled her. The queue ahead of her had entered the bus. She looked glassily at the driver of the bus who smiled at her. As she sat down away from the crowd, the picture of her ordeal flashed through her mind. She was glad to be away from it all.

Five heavily armed men hurried out of a van and made their way into the premises of New Storm newspaper. The driver of the van swung the van around, leaving the engine running and positioning the van at a suitable angle for an easy get-away. Two other men in the van made signs to each other and the driver and whispered slogans. A middle-aged man swung the gate open. The gateman's hands had been tied behind him, his mouth gagged with a piece of cloth. He watched the men in fright. It was a sunny afternoon and the heat made the men sweat profusely.

The building was almost deserted because most of the writers had gone out to cover different assignments. Iye Jillo and a few others were left in the office. She had been seated at her desk all day, battling with different reports she had to submit to her editor. She looked at her watch and realised she had been glued to her chair for over three hours. She decided to stretch her aching legs at the same time the hefty men made their way into the premises. She walked to the toilet, puffing on a cigarette. Then, she heard a door bang and, before she could turn back to find out what was happening, she heard voices, strange male voices giving orders to her colleagues as they screamed for help. With shaking hands Iye removed her shoes, quietly dashed for one of the toilets and locked herself inside. Letting down the toilet seat she climbed onto it and bent to conceal herself as best as she could. She listened to muddled voices and hurried steps as her office was torn apart. Her colleagues cried, screamed and shouted as they were beaten and roughly handled. Trembling, she waited, praying fervently not to be caught.

One of the men gave orders for a thorough search of the premises. Iye trembled as another man went from one room to another. Her heart raced the moment he opened the door leading to the toilets. Almost immediately, she heard the door close behind him. Tears welled up in her eyes, and not until almost an hour later, when she was sure no one was left on the premises, did she attempt to leave the toilet.

Back in her office, the sight was shocking. Drawers had been turned upside down, torn papers littered the floor, files were scattered on the tables and wires had been ripped out. Most of her colleagues had been kidnapped. A few were tied to their tables. Iye ran out, screaming for help. A muddled voice outside caught her attention as she dashed out of the building. It was the gateman. He had been beaten to a pulp and one of his wrists had been slashed.

The incident marked the beginning of an unstable life for Iye and many of her colleagues, who were constantly threatened. In a similar incident, detectives from the Criminal Investigation Division (CID) searched their office and apprehended the publisher, editor and news editor. The arrests were motivated by an article in an issue of New Storm that quoted portions of an alleged telephone conversation between a major in the Nigerian-led West African peacekeeping force (ECOMOG) and a colonel in the Revolutionary United Front (RUF) rebel forces of Sierra Leone. Three journalists were charged with publishing alarmist news under the Emergency Press Law. In a press release issued after that, ECOMOG rejected the report, claiming that the alleged conversation never took place. Subsequently the lives of journalists were constantly in danger.

Sitting at her desk one beautiful morning a few years after Iye had settled in Ireland, she stared into space as she reflected on thoughts that continually bit hard into her heart. I broke her thoughts as I made my way into her office that morning and my smile seemed to bring her back to life. For someone full of fun, pouring out her heart to me was as easy as reciting a nursery rhyme.

The fourth out of five children, Iye grew up very attached to her immediate younger brother, Christopher. Her father was an accountant and her mother a nurse. She had her primary school education at St. Anne's Irish school on House Street in Freetown, Sierra Leone, after which she was admitted into Annie Walsh Memorial Secondary School, a British school located in the centre of the city of Freetown.

Annie Walsh Memorial Secondary School was one of the biggest and best and every girl's dream at that time. The school began with a vision to educate young African girls in the pursuit of excellence in all areas, including high academic performance, sound discipline and a solid Christian foundation. The general assembly was organised by nuns and Catholic fathers. Iye remembers vividly how she recited the catechism with the other students at the assembly. The catholic nuns were the administrators while the teachers were mostly Sierra Leoneans. After the assembly, students would go to their different classes where they were taught one subject after the other and, later in the day, they would take part in games. The routine was the same year after year. Iye's father made it a duty to take his children to school daily. He had made a deliberate decision for them to attend Irish primary schools and British secondary schools, even though he was a Protestant by faith and an Anglican by denomination. He wanted them to understand the different types of faith in Christianity. Sometimes, Iye found the two forms of worship confusing.

Between 2 p.m. and 3 p.m. every weekday, school was over. At home there was always a delicious bowl of food prepared by Iye's mother, which all her children ate together from one bowl. Her father would then go through their homework with them. After that, they rested, read or sat down to tell fairy tales. Such was a typical primary-school day for Iye. A few times when the whole class was punished for misbehaving, they would all be given warning letters to show their parents. On occasions like that Iye would hide the letter or cry to her mother, who knew the trick of getting it across to her father who made it a duty to regularly update himself with their teachers and tutors insisting he had to know how each of his children were progressing.

For ten years the daily routine for Iye was rarely different. Spending seven years between 1984 and 1992 in an all girls secondary school was an exciting experience for her. Her school principal, Madame Grace Williams, touched her life in many ways. She was an educationist from an influential family who always told the girls to hold themselves high and sit straight. She made a good impact in the life of Iye and many others because of the personal interest she took in all her students and teachers. She was fond of telling her students 'Do not grovel', a sentence that today still echoes in Iye's mind.

The five years in secondary school were exceptionally good for Iye, who was among the best in her class. But in the two years of her advanced level education, around 1990, when rumours of the war from Liberia started filtering into Sierra Leone, her education became shaky. Because of the war, many of the experienced teachers were transferred from her school to the United Kingdom and the Unites States of America. Anxious questions were being asked about what the future of young children in Sierra Leone would be, especially when a national call came for young men and students to join the army to defend the borders of their country from neighbouring countries such as Liberia.

About 1991, the refugee movement became visible in Sierra Leone. The reality of the war began to dawn on many when Liberian refugees started trooping into Sierra Leone. Around that time Iye was admitted into Fourah Bay College, Sierra Leone, an establishment intended to provide its pupils, the children of the freed slaves and liberated Africans, with opportunities to obtain training in basic skills needed to survive, and also to train those who displayed the requisite aptitude as teachers and priests.

At the university, Iye graduated with a Bachelors of Arts in media and psychology. During the course of her study, life was not too smooth for her because of the instability created by the war and because her parents were on the verge of getting a divorce. Three of her elder sisters, who were already in the UK, provided her with financial support, as the family structure had been affected at home. Her father kept having affairs and, even though his children tried talking some sense into him, he refused to listen.

Iye could never understand her father's betrayal and this was reflected in her relationships in college. She saw most men as irresponsible and never took them seriously.

Campus life for most students was tough and university life for Iye was rough. There were strikes, and the examinations were badly affected.

There were also political upheavals in the country, with a war at hand. Most villages in Sierra Leone like Pendembu, Tongo (very rich in diamonds), Kono, Makeni and many others were already feeling the effects of the war, though Tongo and Kono in particular provided support for lots of students. Students were terrorised by the National Provisional Ruling Council (NPRC), who used the influence of the military in getting them from different college campuses to abide by their wishes. The NPRC were military men whose duty was to safeguard Sierra Leone's border at Liberia. The situation got worse and the instability gave rise to a coup in January 1994. The Sierra Leone head of state was ousted in a palace coup and replaced by his deputy by a group of final year students who had joined the army. The new government announced a dusk-to-dawn curfew and suspended plans for the proposed February vote to return the country to civilian rule.

After graduation Iye's interest in journalism grew. With her sisters and mother supporting her financially, she began to build her career in freelance journalism. She worked mostly in border countries, which were either directly or indirectly affected by the war. At The Gambia newspaper, she worked as a freelance regional reporter, and she also reported at Guinea Conakry Town in Ghana. Eventually she got full-time employment with the New Storm newspaper, a newspaper that dealt with politics, economy and finance.

Most of the editorials of the paper at that time focused on the political instability of the country. The chief editor and publisher of the paper, Eddie Smith, took Iye under his wing in the editorial team, where she worked, on and off, for two years. Smith began to cover certain districts for the BBC after the military coup. He also worked for the independent Vision newspaper. Iye reported on politics, as well as arts and culture. She was based in the provinces, moving with the

ECOMOG (the Nigerian-led West African peacekeeping force) and sending news to her editor for publication.

Election time came. Sierra Leoneans had hopes once again but rebels began to revolt, to disrupt the plans. They killed and maimed people at will, going from village to village. At one time, they beheaded twenty farmers and hacked the hands off five other people in a village in an attempt to force the government to cancel the polls. Despite this, the primary elections were held. The rebels did not give up. After the elections, they amputated the hands of 50 villagers who voted in the election and threatened more amputations on anyone who voted in the coming run-off election. Voters had their eyes poked out, legs, arms or noses severed, or were killed outright in retaliation for voting. The rebels also used hot irons to brand the words 'no election' on villagers' backs. The situation was pathetic. Women and children wailed all day, praying and begging for help to come.

Things remained the same until after the election, which was pronounced free and fair by international observers. The military handed over to the civilian government and the swearing-in was followed by a public ceremony in Freetown's main stadium while tens of thousands of supporters celebrated in the street.

Again, things appeared to be normal, but only for a very short time. Fighting led by rebels began again and the whole country became their target. Little towns and villages that had been left out started to feel the war. Women, children, the old and the sick were either rendered homeless or killed outright. An Irish Roman Catholic Missionary, Edward Kerrigan, who had been based at the Christian Brothers Mission in a town named Bio for five years, was also killed in a rebel ambush along Freetown-Bio road. He died when his car came under heavy gunfire.

The situation in the country got worse, with journalists being the target of not only rebels but also the government forces. Their lives were repeatedly threatened and most of them had to report stories while in hiding. Many of them were arrested and wrongfully charged with publishing false reports. In 1997, three journalists were remanded to prison after their application for bail was denied. The Committee to Protect Journalists (CPJ), a non-partisan group of journalists dedicated to the promotion of press freedom worldwide, protested at the harassment of journalists and urged the government to guarantee the protection of the media's right to practise its profession freely and safely. They described the arrests as grave attacks on press freedom and a blatant violation of their right to hold and express opinions and ideas.

By May of the same year, soldiers overthrew the new civilian government one early morning, when heavy shooting was heard in Freetown from the direction of the State House and military headquarters. Freetown was then put under a dusk-to-dawn curfew, with coup leaders threatening that looters, military or civilian, would be shot on sight. The country's borders were sealed and the airport and the seaports were ordered closed. Gunfire continued into the evening hours as looting soldiers moved around the city in vehicles they had commandeered from the United Nations, NGOs, the government, religious missions, the Red Cross and civil servants and members of parliament. There was panic as people tried to escape. Twenty people drowned while trying to flee across a river after rebels attacked them while they were in church. In another situation, attackers in military uniforms broke into a house, waking the owner who killed one of them with a machete. The others opened fire, killing a woman and her four-year-old son. Following these attacks, about 1,5000 Sierra Leonean refugees crossed the border within ten days. There were rumours the army was responsible. The government was determined to crack down on army indiscipline. In an effort to do this, they executed soldiers who had been convicted either of collaborating with rebels or of armed robbery with violence or murder. About forty of them were sentenced to death and others given jail terms ranging from five to fifty years.

One afternoon in May 1998 as Iye listened to the news, the BBC reported that the editor of New Storm, Eddie Smith, had been killed when junta forces ambushed an ECOMOG military convoy. An ECOMOG soldier and five militiamen were also reported to have died in the attack. By the time the news was over, Iye's eyes were red and swollen shut. She couldn't control the tears. Her mentor and the only person who gave her hope for the future was dead. She almost gave up her career when, a month after that, police raided the offices of newspaper houses in Freetown, including hers, arresting all their editors. The arrests had followed a warning by the Minister of Information, Communication, Tourism and Culture that the government was prepared to crack down on editors who published disturbing reports. More arrests were made and many officers, carrying warrants signed by the Attorney General and Minister of Justice, searched and raided newspaper offices routinely, giving the excuse that they had received anonymous phone calls that bombs had been planted on their premises.

By 1999, Sierra Leone had become the world's most dangerous country for journalists, with a total of ten journalists killed in the line of duty. The combined rebel forces of the Revolutionary United Front (RUF) and the Armed Forces Revolutionary Council (AFRC) viewed all journalists as enemies. In a bloody three-week operation in Freetown, rebel forces executed at least eight journalists, some together with their families. This happened shortly before being ousted by the Nigerian-led West African peacekeeping force ECOMOG. They also damaged and destroyed the offices of several news organisations, including those of the Independent Newspaper, Concord Times and Standard Times. Many journalists were abducted or went into hiding, and some fled into exile. Their whereabouts could not be confirmed for several months. Journalists were being attacked by virtually every party in the conflict, including successive military juntas, rebel forces, civilian governments, peacekeeping troops and, until early 1997, even South African mercenaries fighting in Sierra Leone.

Civilians in general continued to complain of harassment and extortion by armed rebels and even after a peace agreement was made to protect journalists, some of them still received death threats while others were forced to change houses daily for fear of being attacked.

Iye became more depressed and less devoted to her job when her colleagues were being kidnapped, harassed and killed daily. For months she hid herself in different towns, moving when she sensed her life was in danger. She squatted with some of her friends and colleagues. She lost most of the things she had kept and treasured for years while hopping from one place to another. As the war got worse, she became depressed and cried constantly, wondering what to do with her life. At some point she felt there was no hope or future for her in Sierra Leone any more. She got several threatening calls and letters.

She ran every time she suspected being trailed and, at some point, her brothers too began to get threatening calls because they refused to reveal Iye's whereabouts. Their mother felt that her children were no longer safe and began to emphasise the need for them to leave the country. She was particularly concerned about Iye because her profession put her life more at risk.

Iye began to map out a plan. She thought of ways to go about it and, every time she came to a conclusion, her plans centred on Guinea Conakry Town, in Ghana. Ghana was the closest and safest place she could hide, until she was able to find a more suitable place to go. She was ready to go wherever fate took her and ready to face whatever came her way. Guinea Conakry already hosted 190,000 Sierra Leonean refugees who had begun to arrive after the onset of the rebel war in 1991. Guinea had several times appealed to the International Commission for assistance to cope with the influx of refugees. The massive and sudden presence of these refugees had caused public health problems. There was a shortage of drinking water and some had already died of cholera. But despite that, most of the refugees preferred to stay there than go back to a country where life had no value.

With her mind made up, Iye got up one evening, packed some small luggage and left with a group of people for Guinea Conakry. As they made the journey there, a flicker of hope stirred in her. Soon after her arrival, Iye approached the Sierra Leonean Embassy, hoping to get some form of papers for identification purposes. After going through a lot of difficulties, she eventually got a travel certificate with attestation papers. She began to get accustomed to her new environment and, though living was not particularly comfortable, she was at peace with herself.

After spending three months tackling different obstacles and difficulties, between July and August 1999, Iye's sisters in the UK arranged for her to leave Guinea Conakry. They made frantic efforts to get her a British visa so she could join them but Iye, with many others who had also applied for visas, was bluntly refused by the UK Embassy. The British consular officer was particularly difficult and very uncooperative because of his belief that the airlifting of many Sierra Leoneans from Guinea earlier that year to Britain had attracted an influx of more people into Guinea claiming to be Sierra Leoneans.

When everything else failed, Iye's sisters made alternative arrangements for her to fly to Paris, from where she came to Ireland.

As Iye raised her head that day in her office, I knew it was time for me to stop. I made a final full stop on my notepad, shook her hand and wished her well in her new life.

Rwanda at a Glance

History: The name Rwanda once evoked images of the amazing mountain gorillas of the Parc Nacional des Volcans and breathtaking mountain views. The earliest known inhabitants of what is now Rwanda were the Twa pygmies, an ethnic group that still lives in the country today but makes up only a paltry 1% of the population. The Twa held sway over much of the mountainous terrain until around the 11th century, when Hutu farmers migrated into the region and displaced them. A few hundred years later the Hutus were subjugated by the warrior-like and pastoralist Watutsis who came down from either Ethiopia or Southern Sudan in the 16th century and forcefully impressed their harsh system of feudalism on the area. Nothing much changed in Rwanda until the Belgians found it administratively convenient to not only uphold but also increase the power of the Tutsis in Rwanda, allowing the tribal minority to enjoy even fuller control of the country's bureaucracy, military and education systems over the large Hutu population. Things started unravelling for the Belgian-backed Tutsi leadership in the late 1950s, when Hutus started demanding an improvement in their living conditions and an easing of their ethnic suppression. The response from a newly empowered and particularly ruthless Tutsi clan in 1959 was to murder every Hutu leader they could find. But rather than terrify the Hutus into submission, the plan backfired and generated a Hutu uprising in which an estimated 100,000 Tutsis were massacred. The civil violence ironically forced the Belgians to institute political reform that led to the declaration of Rwanda's independence in 1962, which was accompanied by the country's first officially recognised Hutu government. However, tensions between the two dominant groups remained high and the inter-tribal killings continued. In 1972, tens of thousands of Hutu tribespeople were massacred in neighbouring Burundi and in the aftershock of the incident the Rwandan prime minister was overthrown by his army commander, a major general. The major general somehow managed to keep a lid on Hutu-Tutsi hatred for another 18 years, keeping the country's depressed economy afloat by sidestepping the burden of huge internationally financed debt. Unfortunately in 1990 the country imploded. On 1 October, Rwanda was invaded by about 5,000 well-armed Tutsi exiles, collectively called the Rwandan Patriotic Front (RPF), from their base in Uganda. Within days, the Hutu army (bloated with extra troops from France, Belgium and Congo/Zaïre) went on a rampage against the Tutsi and any Hutu suspected of collaborating with them. Thousands of people were slaughtered and, regardless of the human toll, the RPF tried again in 1991 and, after a failed ceasefire, another attempt was made in 1992.

A peace accord was signed between the government and the RPF but the peace that was accorded unfortunately turned out to be a very short one. In 1994, Rwanda became the scene of the worst humanitarian crisis since World War II. Over three million Rwandans fled the country to refugee camps in neighbouring countries. The killing spree abated only when the United Nations Security Council finally decided enough people had died to warrant the time-consuming and generally inconvenient deployment of international troops. That same year a Government of National Unity, which was established by the RPF, began to try and deal with the poverty and ethnic violence that still faced a million Tutsi refugees in border camps and insurgencies from Hutu extremists now based in Congo (Zaïre). Considering the country's track record and the history of bloody unrest in the region, Rwanda may not be entirely free from ethnic conflict or live harmoniously with all of its African neighbours.

Economy: Whatever progress Rwanda was making to climb out of the pit of its colonial past was undermined by the collapse of the value of its export commodities: tin and, more important, coffee. Until 1989 when coffee prices collapsed, coffee was, after oil, the second most traded commodity in the world. That year negotiations over the extension of the International Coffee Agreement, a multinational attempt to regulate the price paid to coffee producers, collapsed when the United States, under pressure from large trading companies, withdrew, preferring to let market forces determine coffee prices. This resulted in coffee producers glutting the market with coffee and forcing coffee prices to their lowest level since the 1930s. While this did little to affect coffee buyers and sellers in wealthy countries, it was devastating to the producing countries like Rwanda and to the small farmers who produced it. The sudden drop in income for small farmers resulted in widespread famine, as farmers no longer had any income with which to purchase food. The consequence for the Rwandan state elite was just as devastating because the money required for maintaining the position of the rulers had come from coffee, tin and foreign aid. With the first two gone, foreign aid became even more critical and the Rwandan elite needed more than ever to maintain state power in order to maintain access to that aid. Maintaining access to aid, however, particularly from multilateral organisations, required agreeing to financial reforms imposed by those organisations. In September 1990, the IMF imposed a structural adjustment programme on Rwanda, which devalued the Rwandan franc and further impoverished the already devastated Rwandan farmers and workers.

The prices of fuel and consumer necessities were increased and the austerity program imposed by the IMF led to a collapse in the education and health systems. Severe child malnutrition increased dramatically and malaria cases increased 21%, due largely to the unavailability of antimalarial drugs in the health centres. In 1992, the IMF imposed another devaluation, further raising the prices of essentials. Peasants up-rooted 300,000 coffee trees in an attempt to grow food crops and partly to raise money but the market for local food crops was undermined by cheap food imports and food aid from the wealthy countries. The economy has since been resurrected.

Population: The population of Rwanda is estimated to be 9.5 million The Hutus comprise around 80% of the population, the Tutsis make up less than one-fifth of the population and the Twa pygmy group make up the remaining 1% of the population.

Languages: Kinyarwanda is the language most widely spoken in Rwanda. English and French are pretty much tied for second place linguistically. Swahili is also used in some parts of the countryside.

Culture: International awareness of the two main ethnic groups in Rwanda is unfortunately mainly based on the fact that one tried to wipe out the other in the mid-1990s after a long period of cultural suppression and tribal bitterness. However the vibrant cultures and traditions are gradually gaining ground again.

Ethnic groups: There are just a few ethnic groups in Rwanda. The Hutus make 80%, the Tutsis 19% and the Twas just about 1%.

Religion: Christianity dominates in terms of religion, adhered to by two-thirds of the population. Tribal religious beliefs occupy another

25% of Rwandans, while 10% of residents are practising Muslims.

Food: Kigali offers a good number of eateries, clubs and liquid refreshment joints and is a good place to indulge the senses. A Non-Governmental Organisation (NGO) satisfies an array of restaurants clustered around Place de l'Independence (Independence place) that serve up everything from regional African fare, upmarket French dishes, Italian, Greek, Indian and Chinese cuisines. Ethnic regional staples like tilapia fish, Nile perch or the ubiquitous Ethiopian dishes of wat and injera (fishes) are in abundance in Rwanda.

Tourist Attraction: Rwanda's captivating natural features offer some hard-to-beat experiences, from the mountain gorillas in the reopened Parc Nacional des Volcans to the hundreds of species of trees and birds in the magnificent rainforests of Nyungwe. Gorilla tracking is the activity of choice in the Parc Nacional des Volcans, where Dian Fossey spent 18 years studying the impressive and fascinating beasts until her murder by poachers in 1985. This national park reopened in July 1999 after years of civil violence in the surrounding area and is once again the place in east Africa for observing mountain gorillas. The beautiful bamboo- and rainforest-covered slopes of this volcano-crowded national park is in Rwanda's northwest. The mountain gorillas of east Africa are now thought to number barely 600 and are distributed throughout national parks along the shared borders of Rwanda, Uganda and Congo (Zaïre).

Kigali: Kigali city is small but rates high on the attractiveness scale, dotted as it is with a wide variety of colourful flora and with a number of viewpoints looking out over Rwanda's other 999 hills. Besides the natural splendour of its verdant location, there's not a lot of sightseeing material in Kigali.

Gisenyi: Relaxation is exactly what attracts the wealthier Rwandans, experts and travellers looking to splurge to the lakeside resort town of Gisenyi. Situated on the eastern shore of the enormous Lake Kivu, Gisenyi is stuffed full of manicured villas, salubrious hotels and the requisite nightclubs. Gisenyi owes its existence to the stunning Lake Kivu, which provides it with expansive views and swim-able, sunbath-able sandy beaches. To the south of town is the impressive 328 foot-high waterfall Les Chutes de Ndaba. A swivel to the northwest reveals the magnificent 11,381 foot-high Nyiragongo volcano.

Butare: From presentations of Rwanda's prehistory and ethnic beginnings to vibrant cultural performances, there is plenty in Butare to exercise the mind. The Musee National du Rwanda is a huge and amazing Belgian-donated architectural treat that houses a wide variety of archaeological and ethnographical displays. This museum, which is regarded as the centrepiece of Butare, ranks as one of the best museums in the east African region. The museum is also the facilitator for a traditional Rwandan dance troupe, which puts on a spectacular full-costumed and heavy-rhythmed show when there.

Nyungwe Forest: The Nyungwe Forest is a mountainous 378-square-mile (970-square-kilometre) protected rainforest reserve in southern Rwanda. There are over 20 kilometres of pristine hiking trails in the area, exposing walkers to enormous hardwood stands, numerous waterfalls and an mind-boggling variety of other trees, birds and insects (including some dazzling species of butterfly). The main attraction of Nyungwe is the proliferation of black-and-white Columbus monkeys. The mammals wander around in huge troupes, some of which are made up of over 300 agile individuals.

CHAPTER SEVEN

Mary
Rwanda

It was about 9 p.m. A black van made its way through the village to the city, going at a maddening speed. It swerved from one side of the road to the other as the driver tried to avoid potholes. Cramped inside it were people who had been captured. They were mostly women and children. It was so dark inside that they could hardly see each other. The only tiny window that served as a source of ventilation had bars wired across it. There were no seats and, each time the van went into a pothole, its occupants were thrown in different directions. Heads banged and hands stretched out for anything that could be grabbed to keep them from falling. The air in the van was humid, smelly and uncomfortable. Young children fainted from lack of fresh air. Women cried as their babies coughed and choked. The people in the van banged on the barrier that stood between the driver's seat and the back of the van. The driver drove on, as if he was under some spell. He had been given instructions to make the journey as fast as possible, so he could go back to pick more victims. If he disobeyed the orders or made a simple slip, he would pay with his life.

The tyres screeched as the driver brought the van to a final stop in front of two tall gates. A man behind the gates peeped through a tiny hole in the gate. In a moment, the massive gates flung open and the driver drove the van into a large compound. He stopped the van in front of a bungalow. The gates roared to life again, shutting their jaws with a loud bang. The fence around the bungalow was the same height as the gates and through it ran electrified barbed wire.

The bungalow looked deserted. Silence hung over the camp.

The journey to the camp had lasted three gruesome hours. Women cried as they were dragged out of the van. Some of the people who had travelled in it had died on the way of suffocation and stampede. Dead bodies were also dragged out of the van. Those who had escaped death shook with rage and vomited at the sight of the dead ones. Like slaves in the nineteenth century, they followed the orders of their captors as they were marched into different rooms in the bungalow. Inside, they

114

were divided into different groups and locked inside rooms that had oil lamps as the only source of light.

Mary sat down on the floor in a corner and watched as other frightened faces joined her. She was sick and tired. She was also hungry. She leaned against the wall and stretched her legs. She stared into space, praying for help to come.

A loud bang outside the camp cut into her thoughts, bringing everyone in the room to life. Everyone scrambled to the window to see what was happening.

A man had been tied to a tree. He was almost naked and had been badly beaten. Blood tickled down one side of his face over the caked dried blood on his cheeks. Across from him stood three armed men. They looked indifferent, vicious and dangerous. They had iron whips, long ropes, knives and guns in their hands. Down the line was another man seated on a wooden stool, barking out orders to the three-armed men. The man tied to the tree was crying, begging the men to spare his life. His cracked voice broke into sobs. His body shook in pain and agony.

One of the men moved closer to him and told him he had a last chance to tell the truth or his throat would be cut. Another, grinning, said he would be glad to cut off his fingers. The man kept pleading and begging to be released. The third man told him he would shut his mouth permanently for him if he didn't shut it that minute. The sobbing continued.

After a few minutes, the man on the wooden stool got up, dragged his feet as if they were made of iron and walked to the three armed men. Looking at the armed man with disgust, he whispered something, turned and walked away, still dragging his feet behind him.

Two of the men moved forward: one of them began to whip the man tied to the tree while the other picked up a bottle and poured the contents on his back. The man screamed and kicked, pleading for mercy. Each lash on his back was like a stab in the women's chests. Tears rolled down their cheeks. They looked at each other. No one moved or said anything. Then the man's body went limp.

Someone tapped Mary's shoulders. She was startled. A woman was asking if she wanted to eat anything. It was one of her neighbours who had been captured the same time as her. They had been held captive for almost two weeks. They had all been brought into a former hospital building that had been turned into a temporary camp. Everything appeared to be at a stand still. She shook her head at the snack her neighbour offered her. Tears rolled down her cheeks. More frightened children and women were being forced into the room.

A blanket of sorrow hung over the city with broken windows, smashed doors and battered roofs. Clothes, shoes and other personal effects littering the streets told the tale of the struggles of the previous night.

Curled up in one corner, Mary covered her ears with her hands to shut out the screams of children and women who were being forced into the room. Everyone was scared. It was chaotic. Outside the room, she could hear muddled voices. She listened but all she could make out was a particular command being repeated for more people to be captured.

Rwanda had been taken over by rebels. Two ethnic groups, the Batutsis and the Bahutus, were at each other's throats, killing and maiming at will. Mary and many others were too young to understand the reason behind the chaos. The war had been so sudden and so unexpected that no one had had time to think or prepare.

Mary looked around the room again, trying to pick out her cousins and other familiar faces. The only faces she could recognise were those of her neighbours. Though no one said anything, the looks on people's faces said it all. Some showed tiredness, some shed tears, some looked pale and others looked hopeless. Mary could smell trouble, fear and uncertainty in the air. No one knew to what extent the rebels would go. Away in the town, there was chaos and ethnic fighting between neighbours, children and parents, teachers and pupils and friends. What had started as an ordinary argument had resulted in a tribal dispute, which had slowly turned into a war

Coming to live with her cousin in Ireland was something Mary had always looked forward to, especially after she luckily escaped death when war broke out in Rwanda, a small country in Africa reeking with poverty because of corruption. The moment she stepped on the soil of Ireland her hopes soared. But nine years after, the part of her that was missing was still her source of worry. Mary's heart has been with her parents since she left her country Rwanda. Not being able to see them for so long has made her unstable and unhappy and her only hope is that they will still be there when she eventually has the opportunity of visiting them.

Mary was forced to leave Rwanda when war broke out in the nineties. She was in the middle of her fourth year in secondary school and was still too young to understand the reality of the situation. Until then, she had only read and heard stories about war in other countries.

For some years before Mary left Rwanda, her cousin Martha and her husband had taken the responsibility of taking care of her and sending her to school, to ease some of the burden on the shoulders of Mary's parents. Mary was just settling down with them when war broke out and forced Martha and her Irish husband to leave for Ireland.

Mary was the last child of her parents. There were seven of them in all. Four of them had died, leaving vacuums in the hearts of those they left behind. Mary enjoyed growing up. As the youngest, she was spoilt by her parents and not subjected to the kind of discipline her other sisters had gone through. Every morning they would all get up as early as 6 a.m. to fetch water for the house before going to school. Even when Mary was too young to fetch water, she would insist on getting up to watch the others as they went about their duties at home. The best part was when they prepared for school. Their uniforms thrilled Mary and every time they left her behind to go to school, she cried until she was old enough to join them. The journey to school each day lasted 45 minutes. They loved it because they could chatter and play games on the way.

Mary's father was a farmer who specialised in growing coffee beans. Her parents were poor and uneducated and, because her father did not appreciate the value of education, he brought his children up not caring if they were educated or not. Right from when they were young he taught them how to grow, prepare and sell coffee beans, which fetched him just enough money to feed them and buy them a few clothes.

Mary's mother was a housewife and, though she wasn't literate, she insisted on her children having a good education. With her powerful influence, she put them on an educative path in life.

After their primary education, she made sure they all went to a secondary school. Unfortunately, her financial situation was poor so she withdrew some of them from school. Those who were fortunate to finish secondary school left the house as soon as they were through in search of greener pastures, to seek a better life and get married. As the youngest, Mary was left alone with her parents. She went to school alone and at lunchtime she would go home to prepare food for her parents and then walk back to school.

As the years went by, Mary's father continued to trade in coffee and his business made good progress. The coffee business was expanding in Rwanda. By the end of 1989, 85% of the Rwandan export economy was already based on coffee. Unfortunately, the international coffee market agreement collapsed in the summer of that year, producing a significant shock not only to Mary's father but also to the Rwandan economy. Things began to deteriorate for all those who dealt in the coffee business. As a result, the military and civil servants who formed the backbone of the government's power base were poorly paid.

It was at this point that Martha offered to take up Mary's education. Mary's mother couldn't take her education any further and her father's business had collapsed.

Mary lived with Martha and her husband in Kigari city in Rwanda. Her education went smoothly until war broke out. Kigari was greatly affected by the war and people were being maimed and killed daily. Their lives became unsafe. As the situation got worse, Martha and her husband decided to leave Rwanda for Ireland. It was a decision they had to take in a hurry. Before they left, they handed Mary over to their friend, who was kind and willing to take care of Mary until she was able to join them in Ireland.

The situation in the country shook the seat of power, giving detractors loopholes to attack and destabilise the country. The political unrest, which led to war and forced Mary and many others to flee Rwanda, had begun when fighting broke out between the different tribes in the country. The two main tribes affected were the Batutsis and the Bahutus. By unifying one of the tribes with the other in opposition, the government tried to quell the unrest. This put the political situation in the country under control. Unfortunately the stability only lasted for a short while. With support and backing from Uganda, the Rwandan Patriotic Front (RPF) invaded Rwanda in 1990. Their stated motivation stemmed from their dissatisfaction with the slowness of the democratisation process. They wanted to either force the president from power or place pressure on him to open political channels for representation of the Batutsi minorities. The invasion led to war and for two years a bloody civil war raged on between the Rwandan government forces and the Batutsi rebels.

In 1992, a ceasefire accord for the peace process as well as power sharing was signed. By 1993, a United Nations mission was sent to Rwanda to monitor the peace accords and their implementation. However in 1994 the presidents of Rwanda and Burundi were killed in an airplane crash. The crash occurred when anti-peace militia groups shot down their airplane. There was chaos in the country and great speculation about who was responsible for shooting down the plane. The two main tribes blamed the incident on each other.

Soon after the plane was shot down, the Bahutu-dominated militias initiated a mass campaign of genocide against the Batutsis. Human Rights Watch and other international organisations speculated that it was the extreme Bahutu elements within that administration, who did not believe the president's efforts to excise Batutsis were sufficient, who had shot down the plane.

In the violence that followed, Rwanda's prime minister and her 10 Belgian bodyguards were all also killed. By July 1994 up to one million Batutsis and Bahutu moderates had been killed by Bahutu extremists. The Rwandan genocide of 1994, compared to the Nazi exterminations during World War II, stands as one of the great human atrocities of the 20th century. Some scholars call it an evolutionary step in mass murder. The ferocity and rapidity of the killing, which took place in about 100 days between April and July 1994, had seen few equals in modern history. The United Nations, the United States, France and Belgium played significant roles in helping the situation.

After the capital of Rwanda was seized, members of its previous government, the armed forces and all others involved in the genocide fled to Zaïre and Tanzania. Mary was already staying with Martha's friend. For many the experience was devastating. For Mary it all started one afternoon as they cooked in the kitchen at home. It was the Easter holiday. A group of people from the Batutsi tribe broke into their house. Violently they captured everyone in the house and its vicinity and took them all into a hospital that had been converted into a temporary camp. A little food and beds were all they got. They went out daily begging for leftovers. They had nothing on them except some worn-out clothes and threadbare shoes on and after a few weeks they were all taken to boarding schools in the north of Rwanda, which had also been converted to camps. There were thousands of them. Rooms were allocated to everyone. Four girls and four men shared a room and cooked together in a common kitchen. With no provision made for care and protection for them, infection spread like a menace, killing hundreds of them.

By this time the Batutsis had taken power. They vandalised and raided the camps, taking away the food and clothing the Red Cross and Médicins sans Frontières (a French charitable organisation) had provided for them. Numerous international reports pointed out that there was no such thing as a refugee in Rwanda during the war. This was because the largest mass killings in the war were of people who took refuge in churches. Most of these churches were burnt to the ground with everyone in them. There were no counts of them. Most shocking was the fact that so many of the people who died were in fact Bahutus killed by other Bahutus.

Batutsis continued to arrest people. They put some in camps and locked the ones who resisted or threatened them in prisons. It was general knowledge that the Bahutus were more educated and enlightened than the Batutsis so the Batutsis harassed anyone who was in support of the Bahutus. The rapidity of the killings was all the more shocking because the majority of people were not shot but hacked to death with machetes or farm tools. Because the reason for a given person being killed was based on ethnicity, women and children were no more spared than men. Many people were killed by their long-time neighbours. Everyone ran for help. Many sought refuge in neighbouring countries. Over two million refugees fled to the northern part of Zaire.

Mary remained in the camp, hoping and praying that her cousin would send for her and her nightmare would end. Stuck in the camp, she began to realise what life really meant. She constantly thought of her parents who were still in the village. She knew they were getting old and likely unable to meet most of their needs. Mary heard nothing of them for a very long time. It was difficult getting any message across to them. A few times, she reached them through some aids in the camp. Many times, news came to her about the old and the aged being subjected to torture and slave labour. Each time such a message came, she prayed for their lives to be spared. Many of her cousins were killed in the war and a lot of her friends and neighbours were missing. Martha kept in touch with her regularly and, though Mary was looking forward to joining her and her husband, leaving her parents behind in Rwanda was a great concern to her. She was also worried she could only speak her native language, very little French with no English at all. Travelling to a country where English was the spoken language spoken made her feel uncomfortable.

After six months, Mary received a flight ticket from Martha and her husband to join them in Ireland. Putting together her small luggage one hot afternoon, she bid Rwanda goodbye.

South Africa at a Glance

History: The humble beginnings of South Africa date to over 500 years ago, when white men first anchored off the shores of South Africa, though Southern Africa has a history of human occupation that goes back thousands of years. For perhaps as long as 10,000 years the Bushmen or San were the only people who inhabited most of South Africa. They were the last survivors in southern Africa of a stone-age culture. They were hunter-gatherers whose existence was governed by the seasons and the movements of the wild game. Black settlers, the Bantu-speaking people, arrived about 4,000 years ago to South Africa, urging their cattle in search of grazing. They were part of a population explosion in central Africa and they needed water and pasture and a land to till. By the late 17th century one of the groups moved into the eastern Cape, setting the stage for the arrival of the white man. The first white people to land in South Africa were the Portuguese. Southern Africa became a popular stop for European crews after Vasco de Gama opened the Cape of Good Hope spice route in 1498 and by the mid 17th century scurvy and shipwreck had induced Dutch traders to opt for a permanent settlement in Cape Town. Towards the end of the 18th century, and with Dutch power fading, Britain predictably jumped in for another piece of Africa. Upheaval in black Southern Africa wasn't only generated by the white invaders. The forced migration in Sotho, a terror campaign masterminded by the Zulu chief Shaka, was a time of immense upheaval and suffering. This wave of disruption through southern Africa left some tribes wiped out, with others enslaved. The first Anglo-Boer war ended in a crushing Boer victory and the establishment of the Zuid-Afrikaansche Republic. The British backed off until a huge reef of gold was discovered around Johannesburg and then marched in again for the second Anglo-Boer war, dribbling with empiric greed. By 1902 the Boers had exhausted their conventional resources and resorted to commando-style raids, denying the British control of the countryside. If a shot was fired from a farm, the house was burnt down, the crops destroyed and the animals killed. The women and children from the farms were collected and taken to concentration camps, a British invention where 26,000 died of disease and neglect. Slavery was a prominent aspect of Cape life for about 200 years. Early settlers were short of labour, and slavery began in earnest in 1668. Slaves came from Guinea and Angola, Delgoa Bay, Madagascar, Java and Malaysia. The newer community absorbed parts of their languages and cultures. There was much mixing of the races, including the black and Hottentots, which created the coloured people. By 1795 when the British took over there were 17,000 slaves.

Although slavery was abolished in 1833, the division of labour on the basis of colour served all whites too well for any real attempt to change. The idea of apartheid or separate development was an uncomfortable political thorn. It had its roots in the introduction of the first slaves and the belief of the Dutch settlers that menial labour was not the lot of the white man, who was innately superior. Segregation became a generally accepted way of life, but it was not by law, and the emergence of a politically aware black middle class led to the growing strength of some organisations. Under apartheid, every individual was classified by race, and race determined where you could live, work, pray and learn. Irrespective of where they had been born, blacks were divided into one of 10 tribal groups, forcibly dispossessed and dumped in rural backwaters, the so-called Homeland. The plan was to restrict blacks to Homelands that were, according to the propaganda, to become self-governing states. In reality these lands had virtually no infrastructure and no industry and were therefore incapable of producing sufficient food for the black population. There was intense widespread suffering and many families returned to squalid squatter camps in the cities from which they had been evicted. Black resistance developed in the form of strikes, acts of public disobedience and protest marches and was supported by international opinion from the early 1960s after 69 protesters were killed in Sharpsville and African National congress (ANC) leaders, including Nelson Mandela, were jailed. Afrikaner identity was again threatened and by the 1920s and 30s times became hard with depression and miners' strikes. Black labour became cheap and the white labour force felt threatened. Constantly there was fear of black encroachment within the whites. In 1961, South Africa withdrew from the British Commonwealth and became a republic. After withdrawing from the British Commonwealth, South Africa became increasingly isolated. Still in the process of reinventing itself, the country is gradually melding into a new society of energy and significance with post-apartheid optimism.

Economy: South Africa is a middle-income, developing country with an abundant supply of resources and well-developed financial, legal, communications, energy and transport sectors. The country has a stock exchange that ranks among the 10 largest in the world and a modern infrastructure supporting an efficient distribution of goods to major urban centres throughout the region. However, growth has not been strong enough to cut into high unemployment and the daunting economic problems from the apartheid era, especially the problems of poverty and lack of economic empowerment among the disadvantaged groups, still remain.

Though poverty still exists alongside riches, the AIDS epidemic is devastating and violence, crime and corruption remain a problem. After the British seized the Cape of Good Hope area in 1806, many of the Dutch settlers (the Boers) trekked north to found their own republics. The discovery of diamonds (1867) and gold (1886) spurred wealth and immigration and intensified the subjugation of the native inhabitants. The Boers resisted British encroachments, but were defeated in the Boer War (1899-1902). The resulting Union of South Africa operated under a policy of apartheid – the separate development of the races. The 1990s brought an end to apartheid politically and ushered in black majority rule. Political violence is a thing of the past and among the vast majority of people there's a desire to get on with building a new nation.

Culture: Although South Africa is the home to a great diversity of cultures, most traditional and contemporary cultures were suppressed during the apartheid years, when their day-to-day practice was ignored, trivialised or destroyed. Known as a multicultural society, most of South Africa's traditional black cultures are based on beliefs in a masculine deity, ancestral spirits and supernatural forces. In the marriage culture, polygamy is permitted and a dowry (Lobolo) is usually paid on the woman. As a symbol of wealth, cattle are used as sacrificial animals. One of the strongest surviving black cultures in South Africa is Zulu and massed Zulu singing at Inkatha Freedom Party demonstrations is a powerful expression of this culture. The Xhosa, known as the red people, also have a strong presence because of the red-dyed clothing worn by most of their adults. The Afrikaners' distinct culture has developed in deliberate isolation; they have been described as wandering with cows and the Bible in the 19th century.

Population: The estimated population of South Africa is 43.1 million, with 77% blacks, 10% whites (60% of whites are of Afrikaner descent, most of the rest are of British decent), 10.5% mixed race and 2.5% of Indian or Asian descent.

Languages: The major languages are English, Zulu, Xhosa, Pedi, Tsonga, Ndebele, Afrikaans, Tswana, Sotho, Swati and Venda.

Religion: South Africa comprises Muslims, Hindus, Christians, Jews and the traditional religions.

Food: Traditional South African cooking combines the best of many cultural cuisines, which have co-existed in the country for over 300 years. Its food is usually of the highest quality. Meat, fruit, freshwater and sea fish and shellfish such as crayfish (rock lobster) and perlemoen (abelone) are considered to be the country's culinary delights and are offered in the country's best restaurants as well as on the tables in many homes.

The main dishes in South Africa are made from maize, sweet potato, gem squash and other vegetables. The Dutch and English influences created practical stews and sausages such as bobotie (a spicy meat loaf), potiekos and well-spiced, much-flavoured boerewors (farmer's sausage). The Portuguese, who were the first to discover South Africa, added peri-peri and fish dishes to the culinary heritage. Furthermore, small communities of Chinese, Italians and Greeks have all contributed new flavours to the South African cuisine. One of the best-loved social traditions is the 'braai' or 'braaivleis', a standard barbeque featuring well-marinated foods (lamb, beef, chicken, potatoes and other vegetables).

Attractions: Cape Town – known as South Africa's oldest settlement and one of the most relaxed cities in Africa – is unequivocally one of the most beautiful cities in the world. It is dominated by a flat-topped table mountain, vineyards and beaches. It also boasts the Castle of Good Hope, one of the oldest European structures in South Africa, a museum and the Victoria and Alfred waterfront. The Roben Island, another big attraction in Cape Town because of its most famous inmate, Nelson Mandela, was a political prison until majority rule.

Durban is the home of the largest concentration of Indian-descended people. It is a big subtropical city in the north-eastern province of KwaZulu-Natal. Here the weather and water stay warm year-round, drawing the crowds to its long string of surf beaches. Also in Durban are an arts gallery and a local history museum.

Johannesburg is the largest city in South Africa, and is also known as Jo'burg, Jozi egoli or the 'City of Gold'. It has wealth, energy and a beautiful climate. Soweto, its main township, is enormous, sprawling with houses, bungalows, huts, shacks and dorms.

The Kruger National Park, which runs along the Mozambique border, is one of the most famous wildlife parks in the world.

The awesome Dragon Mountain in Drakensberg is a basalt escarpment forming the border with eastern Lesotho. It also has superb wilderness trails and the mountain-climbing opportunities are heart stopping.

CHAPTER EIGHT

Mora
South Africa

Mora stared at a picture of South Africa on the wall in her living room. Inscribed on it in her own handwriting were the words: 'In remembrance of my friend Ella who meant so much to me.' The picture reminded her of the days of apartheid. Beyond the frame and the oil painting, she could see students demonstrating with placards. Their faces spelt fear, anger, hunger, sadness and a mixture of other emotions. She saw herself holding her friend Ella with one hand and a placard with the other. They moved with the crowd, shouting slogans of freedom. Far away she saw armed policemen approaching the crowd. The crowd moved on, sometimes breaking into apartheid songs. Then suddenly, she heard a bang, followed by another and then another. She felt a weight pull her down. She looked frantically around. Ella lay in a pool of her own blood. She had been hit.

Mora wiped away a tear that rolled down her cheek and moved away from the picture. Several years had passed. She knew she was slow to heal. She needed something to blank out the picture that stuck in her head, the picture of watching her friend die. She blamed herself for inviting her friend to join in the march. She remembered the events that led to that fateful day. It was meant to start peacefully and end peacefully. It was all smiles when the students of her school planned the march. The idea was to raise burning issues that needed to be addressed. It was meant to be a march for liberation, not for bloodshed. Mora had recalled Ella from an excursion. They attended different schools but she wanted her to be a part of the march. They did so many things together.

I rang Mora's doorbell, bringing her flow of thought to an abrupt end. Her face lit up as she opened the door to let me into her cute apartment. It was in the heart of Dublin city centre. She offered me tea as I sat down, ready to take notes.

Mora was born and brought up in South Africa in the dark era when the country was in the chains of apartheid. As a little black girl, she knew her colour meant restrictions to certain areas. She was aware of people being segregated in schools, buses, markets and hospitals. She was too young to understand. Her parents tried to explain to her several times in a subtle way. Not until she became a teenager did she understand they had always been careful not to plant evil thoughts in her mind. Her mother particularly had suffered discriminations of all forms. She worked as a maid to a white couple for many years. She slaved day and night to make her family comfortable.

As Mora grew up, her parents taught her many lessons about the ideals of life. They taught her to have dignity, self-respect and contentment. No matter what situation they found themselves in, they never complained. Mora thought they were odd. Whenever they were deprived of their rights because of their colour, they took the situation calmly. Mora always wanted to fight for them. She was an only child. She missed not having anyone to share growing up with.

Mora's parents were poor but happy and contented. They lived in a small house, built more or less like a shed, in a densely populated area in the city of Johannesburg. It was a plain house but they loved it. Her father was a farmer and her mother a maid. Every day they trekked for miles to get to their jobs. From a very young age, Mora became used to waking up as early as 5 a.m. every day. Being the only child, her mother would bathe her and prepare her for the day. Every morning, she cooked enough food to last Mora all day. Then she would hand Mora over to her neighbour, Ella's mother, who took care of the two children all day until Mora's mother returned late in the evening. It was a routine Mora's mother did for many years.

Ella's mother was a housewife, her father a petty trader. He traded in used clothes, which he got from neighbouring countries. Ella was also an only child. The closeness between Mora and Ella grew from a very tender age. They saw themselves as sisters. They played, ate and slept together. The two families were close. Mora and Ella adored each other. They were the same age and born in the same month. They had many similarities. They were almost inseparable. Ella's father bought them identical clothes to make them happy. Everyone in the neighbourhood knew them together.

At that time, the criteria for any child to be admitted into a primary school was if the child could touch her ear with her hand placed across her head. Any child who did this easily was admitted into school. It was a sign that the child was mature enough to start school. Most children were not able to do this until they were seven years old and it was not until Mora was eight years that she passed the test.

Mora's primary education went well. She enjoyed trekking with Ella and a few other children in the neighbourhood to the school, which was just a stone's throw from the house. The short walk to school afforded them the opportunity to play games and tell stories on the way. They always learnt new games from each other. They were all brought up to love each other.

Mora and Ella were nick named 'twins'. Their friends were fond of them, their teachers loved them and their parents adored them.

For many years, South Africans of all races struggled to rid the country of apartheid and replace it with a free, non-racial South Africa. This struggle was supported by the international community, which put enormous pressure on the apartheid regime by withdrawing financial support and sometimes boycotting goods produced in South Africa. Unfortunately, before the struggle for democracy came to an end, a lot of damage was done.

It is worth knowing that the struggle for the oppressed majority in South Africa captured the imagination of the people of Ireland in a way that few other causes have done. In 1964, the Irish Anti-Apartheid Movement (IAAM) was founded in South Africa with the sole purpose of helping to end apartheid. The movement was launched at the 'rally to support the international call for the release of Nelson Mandela and his colleagues'. This served as a good starting point for the movement, setting off a series of campaigns for breaking links between apartheid South Africa and Ireland. The movement also maintained very close ties with the African National Congress.

As the IAAM made progress, it made efforts to represent itself in every possible aspect of Irish life. The campaigns were successful. For the over 30 years of its existence, the IAAM involved the entire spectrum of Irish life in its objective to isolate the apartheid regime and to provide solidarity with the people of South Africa, from the parliamentarians, trade unionists, religious organisations and students to the ordinary people. Its support base was anchored among the Irish trade union movement, formalised through the Irish Congress of Trade Unions and the IAAM.

At that time, many people sacrificed their time to support the struggle for liberation by writing letters, attending demonstrations and travelling around the country to hold meetings and address schools, putting pressure on the government to impose sanctions. The IAAM also served as a channel for funds obtained from the International Defence and Aid Fund to aid political trials as well as finance the families of political prisoners.

Throughout its existence, the movement participated in the international action against apartheid with support from the Afro-Asian Peoples' Solidarity Organisation, the United Nations Special Committee against Apartheid and the Liaison Group of national anti-apartheid movements in Europe.

In 1994, there was a free, fair, non-racial and democratic election in South Africa, bringing apartheid and the work of the IAAM to an end. In place of the IAAM, the Ireland South Africa Association was formed. The association was to support the advancement of peace and democracy in South Africa, to bond the friendship between the people of South Africa and Ireland and to assist the reconstruction and development of the country. It took a lot for the IAAM to make a significant impact in bringing apartheid to an end in South Africa and for the Ireland South Africa Association to enforce the reign of peace afterwards. But before these were achieved, events that will forever be remembered by the world were made part of the history of the country.

After their primary education, Mora and Ella were admitted into different secondary schools. The news came as a shock and both of them cried all day as a form of protest. Their parents tried to effect a change but nothing could be done to alter it. At the beginning, the girls cried almost every time they parted ways in the mornings on their way to school. But after a while, they got accustomed to going to different schools. In school, they involved themselves in different activities. Mora was particularly good with school debates while Ella was good in sports. They represented their schools in different competitions.

Mora and Ella grew up to be beauties and brains in their neighbourhood. They made high grades in school and they attracted attention everywhere they went. As they grew older, they were distinctive in their ways and they made plans together. They both wanted to work in the health sector and they planned towards this.

Mora became an active member of the student's representative council of her school. She had been active in school activities even before the council came into existence. She was a brave young girl who stood up for her rights. She hated oppression. She despised cheating or any form of discrimination. She was very outspoken and would face any bully in her class.

In 1976 directives were given to instructors and principals of schools to use Afrikaans as a medium of teaching. Some school boards immediately took against this directive. They did not like the idea. It was a disadvantage to most students. Complaints were launched but nothing was done to change the system. This was the main reason for the protest march that later caused unrest in the country.

At that time rumours went around in urban areas within the English- and Afrikaans-speaking groups that the education of black children was being paid for by the white population. Some school boards objected to this. They asserted that the government secretary for education had the responsibility of satisfying the English- and Afrikaans-speaking people. Accusing fingers were pointed at him. Consequently, as the only way of satisfying the white and black population, another directive was sent, saying that the languages to be taught in all schools should be English and Afrikaans. Heads of schools were warned to adhere to the directives.

The decision did not go down well with many schools. Many students objected to it. In response, a student's representative council was formed. The idea was for the council to serve as a voice and represent the interest of students. The council was also mandated to consult with organisations and individuals of note in the community. Efforts were made by the council to present the needs of the schools to the government. There was no positive response or support from the community. A protest march was planned. The march was meant to be a peaceful demonstration to raise burning issues in the educational sector.

The weekend before that fateful day in June 1976, a meeting was held between the students and members of some notable organisations to finalise the strategy for the march. It was agreed that the reason for the march was psychological liberation. The 'Afrikaans' issue was seen by the students and the community at large as part of a strategy by the

National Party to oppress black people psychologically. They believed ways and means had to be found to counter the threat. They agreed thereafter that fighting a peaceful war of psychological liberation was necessary. With help from organisations and individuals, black secondary school students planned the march. They took to the streets in a massive peaceful demonstration, protesting the introduction of Afrikaans as the medium of teaching in schools. As students, mostly teenagers, protested openly in the streets and townships, white policemen shot them down in cold blood. There was chaos. The students screamed, running for their lives. Placards flew in different directions. Some students fell, drowning in the pools of their blood. There was a stampede.

Mora and Ella ran, holding each other's hands. Confusion and panic set in. Students stumbled on stones and bricks. Many choked as tear gas appeared, from different angles. Others screamed as hundreds of feet ran over them. It was bloody. It was sad. Mora and Ella continued to run. Suddenly, Mora tripped as Ella's weight pulled her down. She looked down. Ella had been hit. She lay in a pool of her own blood.

People wailed as many others followed. There was no control of the deadly weapons. It was alarming.

As violence took over the protest, parents took to the streets to save their children. By the time help came and the violence was quelled, it was too late. Many lives had been wasted. Mora could not understand Ella's death. She could not come to terms with why her own friend had to be one of the victims. In a very quiet but tearful ceremony, Ella was buried. That day a blanket of sorrow spread over the neighbourhood in which she lived. Her parents were devastated. Their only and promising child was gone. It was a nightmare. Mora was in a state of shock for several months. She hardly spoke or ate. Her parents became worried. It was a very painful time for them.

There was immense tension in the months that followed. No one knew what would happen next. There were insinuations and rumours but nothing was concrete. Black students pointed accusing fingers at the whites, claiming the white police got away with killing blacks because blacks had no right to protest. The country went wild with confusion.

Nothing was said or done to those who started the killings. By the end of that year an official and doubtless underestimated figure was given as 575 dead and 2,389 wounded in the conflict.

In an attempt to crush the revolt, a wave of detentions and bans were introduced. But it was too late. Families had been broken and dreams had been crushed.

The violence precipitated a spontaneous uprising led by students, which spread rapidly to all parts of the country. Thousands left to carry on the struggle from outside the country. Many teenagers were among them. They left their homes at night, not telling their parents where they were going or if they would ever return.

The flood of young people into exile after the uprisings served as a serious indictment on all the liberation movements in South Africa. It was believed the movements did not exert enough pressure on the military regime because liberation movements and organisations lacked the capacity or the political will to do so.

After her secondary school education, Mora was admitted into college to study medical laboratory science. The four years in college were challenging to her. She was still badly shaken by Ella's death and this changed her disposition to life. She withdrew, hardly mixing or socialising with anyone. Her only friends were her books. Her devotion to her studies and determination to be independent helped her build a solid foundation towards her goal in life.

At the end of her course, she achieved the best grade in her class. At the graduation ceremony organised by the college, she was honoured with the award for best student of the year. Her words were few. She thanked the college and dedicated the award to Ella.

After graduation, Mora did a year of internship and got a job with the best teaching hospital in Johannesburg. She was happy she could take care of her parents. They were getting old. Her mother was no longer half as active as she used to be. She was confined to the house most of the time.

More trouble erupted. The two main political bodies in the country, the ANC (African National Congress) and the IFP (Inkatha Freedom Party), were always fighting and at loggerheads with each other. People were maimed and killed and fear ruled the lives of others. Rifts between the blacks and the whites erupted daily. The Black

Consciousness organisation, which stood for the truth and vowed to forever uphold it, went through unparalleled repression and hostility. With the spirit of victory, they survived it, going through it with a great measure of pain and dignity. The organisation believed they lost more men and women at the hands of their opponents than any other organisation that fought for liberation. Unfortunately politically motivated violence continued. Blacks were most often the targets. Oppression, injustice and racism continued. Blacks were segregated from buses and other commercial vehicles that whites used. The whites used the double-decker buses and cars. Most blacks were left to use trains and ordinary buses, which served as their only means of transportation. Because the trains were hardly used by the whites, they became a target to get the blacks. It was the easiest way for the attackers to kill blacks in hundreds. There were several robberies. There was violence everywhere. Several gangs halted trains and buses and passengers were attacked at will. People were mugged. Most of the victims were blacks. Using the train became a nightmare for many.

Mora lived with fear and oppression. She was careful where she went and what she did. She felt cheated when she was refused something or deprived of her rights because of her colour. But she kept mute. She didn't want to die. The sound of the gunshots the day Ella died still echoed in her mind. There were lots of shootings and killings on the streets. Many times, Mora narrowly escaped death. Fear ruled most people's lives.

Mora began to plan her career. The instability of the country affected her. She wanted a job in a more interesting and more challenging environment. She needed a change. She wanted a stop to the ugly images that often flashed through her mind. She wanted to get away from it all. She intensified her efforts and trawled health magazines that advertised overseas jobs. She also searched the Internet. After several months, an opportunity presented itself. Mora stumbled on an advert for a job in Dublin. It was in line with her profession. She applied for the job through an employment agency and was offered the job. She was determined to work hard, make money and invest. It took her just two weeks to plan the trip. In June 1998, Mora bid South Africa goodbye, with the hope that things would have taken a different turn when she finally returned home.

Mora looked at her watch. She got up and walked over to the picture on the wall. I knew it was time to go. I thanked her for her time and quietly made my way out.

Today, South Africa can be referred to as one of the youngest democracies in the world. It is sometimes hard to believe the country is a free, non-racial country where people have a say in the government, given its experiences and the violent nature of apartheid. It is also hard to believe that the transformation from apartheid was relatively peaceful.

The dark days may be over but the legacy of apartheid will remain with the people of South Africa for many generations to come.

Kenya at a Glance

History: Kenya, popularly known as an eastern adventure land, is the heart of African safari country, boasting the most diverse collection of wild animals on the continent. The Swahili word 'safari' (meaning journey) wouldn't mean much to most people if it weren't for this east African land. Kenya's history dates back many centuries to the internal diaspora or the early settlements and migrations. Then came the formation of the various language groups that developed their own religions, traditions, governments and ruling systems in which they dictated their way of life and how they managed to keep alive through their trade and occupations. After that came the white settlers, who were followed by the fight for liberation, which gave birth to the Mau Mau freedom fighters and the rise of the Kenyan heroes. The first of many genuine human footprints to be stamped on Kenyan soil were left way back in 2000 BC by nomadic Cushitic tribes from Ethiopia. Four thousand years ago, Kenya had a lot of rainfall. Pastoralists and agriculturalists lived there and practised herding, agriculture and fishing. They migrated slowly from the Ethiopian highlands to northern, central and eastern Kenya. Archaeologists and linguists say that the descendants of these early Cushites do not live in Kenya any more because they moved into central Tanzania as the Dahalos, Mbugus and the Iraqis. The largest Cushitic group was the Somalis who migrated from southern Ethiopia into the tip of the horn of Africa. They lived in northern Somalia as pastoralists and spread gradually northwards, eastwards and southwards. By the 10th century AD, they reached the Indian Ocean coast and lived around Mogadishu. From then on they gradually migrated southwards and westwards to occupy their present homeland in the north-eastern part of Kenya. The Somali speakers called the Garre preceded the Galla in the area between the Juba and the Tana rivers. A second group followed around 1000 BC and occupied much of central Kenya while the rest arrived from all over the continent between 500 BC and 500 AD. The Bantu-speaking people (such as the Gusii, Kikuyu, Akamba and Meru) arrived from west Africa while the Nilotic speakers (Maasai, Luo, Samburu and Turkana) came from the Nile Valley in southern Sudan. As tribes migrated throughout the interior, Muslims from the Arabian peninsula and Shirazis from

Persia (now Iran) settled along the east African coast from the 8th century AD onwards. By the 16th century, most of the indigenous Swahili trading towns, including Mombasa, had been either sacked or occupied by the Portuguese, marking the end of the Arab monopoly of the Indian Ocean trade. The Portuguese settled in for a long period of harsh colonial rule, playing one sultan off against another. The depredations of the Portuguese era and constant quarrels among the Arab governors caused a decline in trade and prosperity. With Europeans suddenly trampling all over Africa in search of fame and fortune, even Kenya's intimidating interior was forced to give up its secrets to outsiders. Until the 1880s the Rift Valley and the Aberdare highlands remained the heartland of the proud warrior tribe, the Maasai. White settlement in the early 20th century was initially disastrous but once they bothered to learn a little about the land the British succeeded in making their colony viable. Other European settlers soon established coffee plantations and by the 1950s the white settlers' population had reached about 80,000. Harry Thuku, an early leader of the Kikuyu political association, was duly jailed by the British in 1922 after the Kikuyu agitated in protest at the economy being dominated by the European settlers. His successor Johnstone Kamau (later changed to Jomo Kenyatta) later became independent Kenya's first president. As opposition to colonial rule grew the Kenya African Union (KAU) emerged and became strident in its demands. Other such societies soon added their voices to the cry for freedom, including the Mau Mau, whose members (mainly Kikuyu) vowed to drive white settlers out of Kenya. The ensuing Mau Mau rebellion ended in 1956 with the defeat of the rebels.

Economy: Since 1993, the government of Kenya has implemented a programme of economic liberalisation and reform. Steps have included the removal of import licensing, price controls, fiscal and monetary restraint and reduction of the public sector through privatising publicly owned companies and downsizing the civil service. With the support of the World Bank, IMF and other donors, these reforms have led to a turnaround in economic performance following a period of negative growth in the early 1990s. Kenya's real GDP grew at 5% in 1995 and 4% in 1996, and inflation remained under control. Political violence damaged the tourist industry, and the

IMF allowed Kenya's Enhanced Structural Adjustment Program to lapse due to the government's failure to enact reform conditions and to adequately address public sector corruption. Moreover, El Nino rains destroyed crops and damaged an already crumbling infrastructure in 1997 and 1998. Long-term barriers to development include electricity shortages, the government's continued and inefficient dominance of key sectors, endemic corruption and the country's high population growth rate.

Population: The population statistics in Kenya reveal that there were about 28,808,658 persons living in the country. Nairobi, Kenya's capital, which was originally little more than a swampy watering hole for Maasai tribes, became a substantial town by 1900. Today it is the greatest city between Cairo and Johannesburg, with a population of 2.5 million and a rapid growth rate.

Languages: English and Swahili are the languages taught throughout the country, though there are many other tribal languages, which include Kikuyu, Luhia, Luo and Kikamba, as well as a plethora of minor tribal tongues. Sheng (a mixture of Swahili and English, along with a fair sprinkling of other languages) is spoken almost exclusively by the younger members of the society.

Culture: In Kenya traditional values have gradually disintegrated over the years as Western cultural values are becoming more ingrained in the society.

Ethnic groups: There are more than 70 tribal groups among the Africans in Kenya and distinctions between many of them are blurred. Some of the ethnic tribes are large, e.g. the Agikuyu, who form a majority of the population within their homeland in the central province. The other large ethnic groups include the Luo, Luhya, Kamba and Kalenjin- There are also some groups of people who form a very small population, such as the tribe of El Molo. Basically Kenya's ethnic groups are divided into three linguistic groups: the Bantus, the Nilotes and the Cushites. The Bantus comprise Embu, Kamba, Kikuyu, Kisii, Luhya, Meru, Kuria, Bukusu, the Nilotes Luo, Iteso, Nandi, Kipsigis, Marakwet, Maasai; and the Cushites comprise Boran, Rendille, Somali. The percentage of each group is Kikuyu 22%, Luhya 14%, Luo 13%, Kalenjin 12%, Kamba 11%, Kisii 6% and others 16%.

Religion: Most Kenyans outside the coastal and eastern provinces are Christians of one sort or another while most of those on the coast and in the eastern part of the country are Muslims. In most remote tribal areas are a mixture of Muslims, Christians and those who follow their ancestral tribal beliefs. The percentages are 35% Protestants, 30% Roman Catholic, 30% Muslims and 5% Animist.

Food: Kenya's cuisine usually consists of stodgy filler with beans or a meat sauce. This is survival food for the locals, a maximum filling-up at minimum cost. The common national dish in Kenya is Nyama Choma (barbecued goat meat). With a thriving local brewing industry, Kenyans love beer almost as much as their dancing.

Tourist attractions: Kenya promises the globe's most magnificent wildlife parks, unsullied beaches, thriving coral reefs, memorable mountainscapes and ancient Swahili cities. Nairobi, Kenya's capital, is lively, cosmopolitan and pleasantly landscaped. For sightseeing, the national museum, the snake museum and the national archives are all interesting and easy to get to. Outside the metropolis are the entertaining Nairobi National Park and the Langata Giraffe Centre. The country's most talked about wildlife park is the Masai Mara National Reserve. Other highly rated parks include Mount Kilimanjaro, the dense Kakamega (with over 330 species of birds) and the fecund soda lakes of Baringo or Nakuru. Kenya is also famous for its game fishing opportunities, white water rafting on the blood curdling Athi/Galana River. Diving, windsurfing and good old beach lazing can also be done around Kenya's coastal towns.

CHAPTER NINE

Joyce
Kenya

Joyce arrived in Ireland not knowing what the future had in store for her. The past was frightening, the present was uncertain and the future was bleak. She needed to focus. She needed a new beginning. Her feelings leaving Kenya were a mixture of pain, joy, hope and uncertainty. Uncertainty because of the doubts in her mind before she made the journey with her husband, John. Even though they had prayed about it, deep down they still had this nagging feeling that something bad was going to happen to them. They had been hunted for months. Several attempts had been made on their lives. There was that anxiety, that constant apprehension. They still carried the fear that they would look back and see people chasing them with machetes and guns. Joyce looked at her new environment in astonishment. She tried to pinch herself to be sure she wasn't dreaming. Little by little the realisation dawned on her that she had freed herself from the barriers her in-laws had erected around her. She looked at John and remembered a letter he had written her when they were in school, a letter she believes triggered the beginning of the trauma that chased them out of Kenya.

A loud bang echoed in the distance, waking the whole neighbourhood. Joyce got up, startled. The clock beside her bed confirmed her fears. It was 3 a.m. She turned to wake her husband John and discovered he was already wide awake. Before she could ask John what was happening, someone outside the house screamed for help. Joyce's heart raced with fear. There were hurried footsteps, then another bang. A few seconds later smoke filled the air. Fire engulfed the house as women and children screamed. Everyone ran out of the house, which Joyce and John shared with other occupants. It was an old bungalow with eight rooms, located in the middle of the village. Four rooms lined each side of the house with a corridor in the middle. The tenants of each of the rooms shared a common entrance in the front and another at the back of the house. They also shared the kitchen, toilet and bathroom, which were located at the back of the house. Some of the rooms housed as many as six people. Joyce carried her son and ran out with John. They stood with the others and watched as what they used to call their home burned down to nothing. The fire brigade came an hour later to quench what was left of the ruins. Men, women and children wailed as they watched their belongings turn to ashes. There were speculations. No one except Joyce and John knew what or who had caused the fire. Joyce couldn't believe John's family could go to the extreme of burning a house they knew other innocent people lived in, all in an attempt to get her. Several times in the past, John's family had warned her that if she did not desist from marrying their son she would be maimed and killed without pity. They had made several attempts in the past to kill her. Each time she had escaped, they reminded her they would not rest until they succeeded in separating her from their son, dead or alive. Once a hit-and-run driver tried to knock her off the road. Another time they tried to kidnap her. When that didn't work, they tried to kidnap John, but somehow all their plans had been futile.

The last attempt they had made was to spray her face with acid. The night before that particular day, she had dreamt that she almost drowned in a well. She had shared the dream with John and together they had prayed for evil to be averted from their lives. As Joyce walked back from the market towards her house, a man who had been shielded behind a pole made a quick move and approached her with a bottle in his hand. Just then a little boy on a bicycle who was being chased by his friend sped past the man, not looking where he was going. The bottle in the man's hand dropped but not before part of its contents spilled on his hands. The man screamed as he watched his hands melt. A crowd gathered to see what was going on. The man confessed he had been sent by John's family to disfigure Joyce's face with the acid.

Joyce ran home badly shaken, trying to imagine what would have happened to her if the little boy on the bicycle had not come to her rescue. The police were duly informed. Statements were taken from Joyce and John but nothing was done. A few months passed. Joyce thought her in-laws had learned from the incident. But they surprised her when they sent another frightful message that their house would be burnt in the middle of the night. Joyce and John dismissed the threat.

They believed since they were sharing the house with many other people the in-laws wouldn't be so evil.

Joyce and John said nothing as they stood and watched the fire brigade douse the remains of the bungalow with water. Joyce stared at the charred clothes and shoes. The only sign showing where their bed had stood was an iron bar Joyce had kept under it the bed for self-defence in case they were attacked at night. What used to be a fridge stood like a black box in a corner. Half burnt papers, bags and cases littered the floor. The tell-tale signs confirmed to Joyce that John's family not only meant their threat to take her life, they would also wipe out her entire family.

There had to be a way out for her and John. Sometimes Joyce blamed herself for not listening to her mother when she was still in secondary school. Her mother had warned her to desist from seeing John when she learnt John's family were religious extremists. Apart from the fact that John's family were conk Muslims who believed no one in their family should marry outside their doctrine, they also believed that Joyce had pushed their son to an early marriage and they were ready to separate them no matter how long it took them.

Joyce grew up in a Christian family in a little village in Kenya. Her mum was a teacher and her father a farmer. She was the second of four children. At 6 a.m. every morning they got up to get ready for school, which was just a few minutes' walk from home. They played games on their way to school every day, and on weekends they helped their father on the farm, even though none of them was really close to him. He was too strict with them. They were closer to their mother, who doted on them. Joyce's parents brought them all up in the Christian way to fear and believe in God. On Sundays the whole family went to church for worship. This helped them grow up to be considerate and loving towards everyone who came in contact with them.

A good science student, Joyce began to build her career and future. She attended boarding school for two years, but left because the school fees were high. Her parents searched for another school and luckily she got a good one, which was a lot cheaper. It was a mixed school where all the male students were day students and all the female's boarders. Joyce enjoyed the big room she shared with many others because, unlike most secondary schools, they were all allowed to cook. It was like a big hall with several double bunks.

Everything went well until she got involved with John. She blames herself, saying that if only she had concentrated on her studies and not been involved with him in her third year, she may not have ended up the way she is today. Joyce and John lived in the same village. Their houses were not too far from each other's. They often met in the playground when they were on holidays. They became friends. It meant nothing to Joyce at first but John kept persuading her until she started seeing him secretly. She knew what she was doing was wrong but youthful exuberance and curiosity got the better of her.

A new chapter in her life opened with a letter John sent to her in school. Joyce had been dating him for a while and, though they both knew they were too young for it, they sneaked out to see each other and exchanged love letters. John wrote so many. He was a good poet. The one that got Joyce into trouble fell into the hands of the deputy principal of the school. His eyes popped. Shock seized him. He couldn't believe his eyes as he read it. He immediately called for the principal and handed over the letter to him. The principal was Joyce's uncle. He found it unbelievable that Joyce, a teenager, was involved with a boy who could write such things to her. Her uncle had always looked at her as a young innocent girl who knew nothing about men and affairs.

It wasn't long before rumours about the letter went round the whole school. Students talked about the dirty things that were in the letter. Joyce was scared that the principal would punish her before the whole school, or suspend her. She ran away to her grandmother's house. She was so naïve: she was sure no one would be able to find her there. After two days the principal sent for Joyce's mother. She was alarmed because she had not seen Joyce. The principal had an idea where she might be. The next day he showed up at Joyce's grandmother's place. Her grandmother let him in, not knowing who was at the door. He expressed his shock and disappointment in Joyce and took her home to her mother. Joyce was ashamed of herself. Before the whole family she promised her mother she would never see John or have anything to do with him again. One of her uncles then suggested she burn the letter he had written to her and send the ashes to him with a letter saying she never wanted to see him again. Joyce obliged. She carried out the instructions before her family. She wrote the letter, wrapped the ashes of the burnt letter in a tissue and enveloped the two and sent it to John. A few weeks later John came rushing to her. It was as if the letter had set a fire burning in him. He apologised to Joyce for all the embarrassment he had caused her, blaming it on childishness. He confessed he was madly in love with her and persuaded her to continue seeing him secretly. Initially Joyce refused to listen and even threatened to tell her parents and the school principal, but when he started buying her gifts and promised their friendship would remain platonic, she gave in to his plea. They started seeing each other again. Like two stubborn children, they sneaked out to see each other for the next few years, until they were out of secondary school.

After her secondary education, Joyce waited at home for a year before her exam results were out. She passed and got admission into a college to read Secretarial Studies for two years. Determined to concentrate on her studies this time, she erased John from her mind and avoided him. Luckily, John also got admission into a college that was far away from where they lived and after he left the village she forgot completely about him. Joyce involved herself only in activities that were connected with her studies. Her parents, friends and sisters where surprised at her new resolution. Her friends, especially, found it strange, wondering why she had chosen to turn a new leaf at the time she had all the freedom she could want. Joyce grew a thick skin against all the nasty things they said. Some said she was scared of mixing with boys because there was nothing left after what John had enjoyed. Others insinuated that she was nursing the hurt because John had dumped her. Joyce ignored everything. She was determined to excel. At the end of her course she did very well. That same month she got an offer to do her work experience with a reputable company.

One evening after work, she decided to buy a few things for her grandmother and drop them off for her before heading for home. It was getting dark when she left her grandmother's. She hated darkness. At the bus stop the queue she met there didn't quell the phobia she had of the dark. She waited. Just as she was about to give up and go back to her grandmother's, she heard her name. The voice sounded familiar. Her head turned sharply to see the man who had called out. He stood there, head up, arms akimbo, his face wearing a challenging grin. Joyce let out a shout of surprise. John stood there, beaming. Joyce had not seen him for over two years. Joyce held her breath, her heart beating fast. For a few seconds they both stared at each other as if rooted to a spot. Then they ran into each other's arms embracing in a long hard kiss and hug. When they eventually caught their breath, they went to a quiet place and sat down to talk. They caught up on old times, not missing out on anything. They talked about their education, their experiences in the last two years, their families and, lastly, about themselves.

From the moment John set eyes on Joyce again he made up his mind to win her heart. They had met by chance, something he called 'a meeting ordained from above'. He appealed to her never to avoid him again, promising to cherish her for life. He apologised for misleading her when they were teenagers and promised to make up for all the wrongs he had done. Joyce stared at him, confused. She realised she loved him more now that he was a grown adult. She admitted that they had both been foolish when they were young and agreed to start with a clean slate. They began to see each other more seriously. They started to make plans for a future together. They were sure both parents would be happy for them now, since they were making positive headway in life. But they were wrong.

Joyce shielded her face from the hot sun as she made her way into John's bank building. They were meant to go out for lunch that day and, later in the evening, to their parents, to let them know that they were reunited and planning to get married. They regularly met for lunch in their break time, and after working hours Joyce would either go to John's office or he to hers. Then they would leave for home together and part ways half-way. They were getting to know each other better, love each other more. Joyce was happy. John was pleased. After lunch that day they made their way to Joyce's house. They boarded a taxi. It rattled as it made its way through the evening traffic. Joyce and John sat quietly holding each other's hand. He was happy. She was anxious. She figured he was OK but was not sure if he was weak. A lily-livered man was the last thing she wanted. She couldn't explain why she was so in love with him and why she was ready to stick by him, no matter what happened. She had often asked herself what makes a man so special that a woman will promise to carry a torch for him all her life? She was sure she would carry a torch for John for the rest of her life. She was also sure he would be there for her, always. They were going to Joyce's house together for the first time since they got back together. They rode in silence on the un-tarred road that led to the house. He looked at her and smiled.

A shout from the street broke into their thoughts. It was John's cousin Daisy. She was walking down the street. Even though it was dark, she noticed them in the taxi. She wanted to be sure it was John so she kept calling his name and waving her hands. John waved back. As soon as she was sure it was him, she stopped waving, turned back and went in the opposite direction. Joyce and John arrived at Joyce's home. The reception from her family was warm and welcoming. Joyce's parents were glad to learn John had made great progress in life. John made his intentions known to them. They gave their blessings. A few hours later, they went to John's house. Unknown to them Daisy had gone to report what she had seen. John's parents knew they were back together. They had objected to the association even though they had not discussed it with him. From the moment they knew what was going on, they made up their minds not to support John. They resented the association because they were Muslims and Joyce was from a Christian home.

As soon as Joyce and John arrived at John's home, they knew something was wrong. John's parents were cold and distant. They told Joyce their son would never marry a Christian and walked her out of the house. John was mad at them but all he said fell on deaf ears. From then on, they began to send threatening messages to Joyce to stay away from their son. One weekend, Joyce's mother met John's at a social gathering. John's mother got up as soon as she sighted Joyce's mother and, right before the gathering, screamed and rained abuses on her, warning her to keep her daughter away from her son. Joyce's mother was shocked. After that incident Joyce's mother, who had initially supported her daughter, called and warned her to desist from seeing John. But it was too late. Joyce and John were determined to go on without the support of their parents. They continued to see each other, even though Joyce received more threats. The greater the threats, the more determined they were. John's mind was made up. Several attempts were made by John's parents to stop them seeing each other. They sent letters to Joyce's boss at work, claiming she was dangerous and a threat to the company. In the middle of it all, Joyce discovered she was pregnant. John's parents swore to maim her if she had the child. Despite this Joyce and John got married secretly and moved to another town. More threats came to them but the more they received, the farther away they moved. Joyce's parents suffered too, because Joyce cut them off. She hid her pregnancy from them.

Joyce and John settled to a new life and managed to set up a nice little home. John got a job, which was good enough to keep them going. The parents on both sides began to search for them. Joyce's parents were concerned about their daughter's safety but John's were after Joyce's life. Several times a pastor who lived a couple of houses away from Joyce's parents' house tried to call the two families to reach a compromise. The fact that Joyce's parents were Christians while John's were Muslims made it worse. John's parents wouldn't listen to anything the pastor had to say and when they felt he was bothering them too much they warned him to stay away. When Joyce's parents discovered their daughter was married and expecting a child for John, they tried to persuade John's parents to forgive and forget. They believed their grandchild would unite them. They believed there was no point in trying to separate them any more but John's parents were mad at them. They rained curses and abuses and threatened to kill Joyce if they did not look for a way of getting their daughter away from their son.

It took Joyce and John a while before they realised John's parents had trailed them to their new home. They had sent someone who went around making enquiries about them. Joyce and John had been living there for a year and, just when Joyce thought it was all over, trouble came again. She was heavy, expecting their second child. She was tired of the stress and strain of moving houses. The search for a new place was difficult. John wanted a place where his family would not be able to find them. The instability of moving around began to tell on Joyce. She was reluctant. The sudden moves had cost John his job and they had to live on what he had left of his savings. They approached their church for help. The pastor suggested the best thing for them was to leave the country. It was while arrangements were being made for them to travel abroad that their house was burnt down. Joyce knew this time that John's parents meant every word of their threat and fear engulfed her wherever she went. She knew her life and her children's lives were no longer safe. With nothing left from the burnt house, they moved into an empty shop offered to them by a church member. They got a small mattress for sleeping. They were very uncomfortable. The pastor took their first son, James, to stay with him in his house.

Two months after that, the shop was also burnt. Joyce was ill. She began to have nightmares. The church arranged a temporary place on the church premises for them to stay. It was a distance from the shop. They parked the little of what was left of what they had acquired in years and started out on a journey to yet another home. They had been advised to make the journey in the night to be sure they weren't spotted by anyone. They couldn't afford to take any more chances. Even though Joyce was not due for more than two months, she prayed not to have her baby. For days she had been feeling all the signs of labour and the strenuous walk that night did not help. She was tired, weak and sore from stress.

Joyce and John panted as they climbed the hill towards the church. The distance they had covered was nothing compared to what was left for them to cover. At one point Joyce sat down crying, refusing to go on. But John urged her on, and they finally arrived on the church premises.

Later that week the pastor handed them over to some missionaries who made travelling arrangements for them to leave the country. The church contributed some money for them.

A few weeks after that, Joyce and John came to Ireland and their past became a shadow.

CHAPTER TEN

Moji
Nigeria

Moji sat down and wept for the whole night. She couldn't sleep. Her mind was filled with all sorts of emotions. It was a mixture of joy and pain. She was pregnant, though she believed it was by the wrong man. She had dreaded the thought of not having any children, so she welcomed the pregnancy with heart-felt gratitude to the Most High. But everything else to her was pain. Though the pregnancy made her happy, nothing else did.

Moji's friend Yemi, who had housed her for the few years she had been in England, became very worried. She tried, but was unsuccessful, to calm Moji. Moji had been through so much and she wailed in prayer for the Lord to give her directions. As she planned her trip to Ireland, she was full of uncertainties. She was sad and unsure of the future, because her life was taking on a new dimension.

Moji had ended up living a life completely the opposite of what she had planned for herself. She couldn't help comparing herself to Yemi, who was married and settled in her nice home with her family in London. Yemi was compassionate. She felt bad and she tried to change Moji's mind to stay, but Moji declined the offer. She couldn't stay. She couldn't live and depend on people for the rest of her life. She had to move on, to start a new life, to face the future with a bold heart and fend for her baby.

Moji was a journalist. She had studied first in Nigeria and later completed her course in England. She had a bright future planned. Unfortunately all her hopes and plans were dashed.

Moji had grown up with her parents in a polygamous home. Her mother had five children. She was a housewife who struggled to do petty business to support her family. She traded in foodstuffs. Moji's father had thirteen children but no one could tell they were from different mothers. There was a special bond between them all. There was love and consideration for one another. They all lived together as one big family. Growing up was full of fun though erratic. There were good times and there were bad times. There were times their father's income was far above average and times when it was well below it. For some few years, Moji's father worked as a sales manager in Kaduna, a northern city in Nigeria. The children loved it because he had a big house. They enjoyed the comfort of the house until the civil war in Nigeria broke out. This disrupted their lives and they were forced to leave the north for Lagos, for safety.

Things took a different turn in Lagos, and they ended up all living in one room to survive. It became very difficult for Moji's father to support his children. He was faced with a heavy burden. His children struggled to keep the home together. The situation taught Moji a few lessons about life and made her very independent. Experience taught her to take bold steps very early in life, and this built up her confidence and courage.

Moji believed in her country, Nigeria, as a child. She believed it was a land of discipline and values where dishonesty was frowned upon. She believed that if you went to school and excelled, you would make it in life. Her primary- and secondary-school educations in Lagos were smooth. She had dreams about Nigeria. She hoped for a time when all tribes would be equal and entitled to the same opportunities. Her secondary school especially was fun. She had lovely and exciting teachers who taught her to be hopeful for the future, which she believed would be good as long as she was hardworking and studious. Moji made good grades and after her secondary education she planned for a career in law. Moji's father was strict. He believed in dictating to his children, especially when it came to taking important decisions about life. He insisted Moji read Education. This caused a big conflict, which resulted in her staying at home for three years. She fought the issue with her father for years. She cried to elders in the family and his close friends to make him change his mind. He refused bluntly.

Moji became unhappy. She lost her enthusiasm and initial excitement. She decided to try her hand at petty trading. She made a good start and realised she had a flair for doing business. She sold designer shoes, bags, watches and clothes. She developed a good rapport with her customers and supplied the glamorous girls in the media with her range of designer products. This gave her the opportunity of making money and contracts through them. She began to love the media profession and all the glamour that came with it. She woke up to the reality of a good education. She was tired of wasting her life and potential. She decided to try for a career in the media. She put her savings together. With a burning urge in her, she left the house one day to register at the Nigerian Institute of Journalism.

Studying journalism was much more exciting to Moji than trading. Her two years in school were rewarding. She had the opportunity of meeting top government dignitaries. With a diploma in journalism, Moji got an offer to do her work placement at the Punch newspaper, one of the best newspapers in Nigeria.

After her work experience, Moji left Punch and went to England to complete her studies. In England, she got a higher diploma in journalism. Throughout her stay in England, Moji worked part time so she could support herself. After her course, her old childhood courage began to come back. Her idealism almost flew out of the window when she saw how Nigerian politicians came to England to squander Nigeria's money. Moji refused to be discouraged. She returned to Nigeria to serve her country. She believed Nigeria still had a chance to survive if everyone contributed positively. She was happy to find the country's leader enforcing discipline in all sectors. The head of state was feared for his strict rules and 'War against Indiscipline'. No one tried any form of indiscipline. Market women, students, traders, professionals and even government officials were wary of what they did. Discipline reigned and sanity returned to the country.

The National Youth Service Corp (NYSC) is a compulsory one-year programme for every university or college graduate in Nigeria. It was designed for fresh school graduates to serve their country and to make their contribution to the government and its economy.

Moji did her NYSC with the National Sports Commission. The pay was nothing to write home about but she was happy. She loved the exposure and enlightenment it gave her. She worked directly with many journalists who had made good names for themselves in the country. Apart from reporting at the sports commission, she also contributed as a freelance journalist to several newspapers and journals. Things turned sour when the country's economy became shaky. There was inflation. An average earner could no longer cope with the situation. A distinct line was drawn between the poor and the rich. The middle class was forced out. Students, traders and ministry workers took to the streets, demanding their rights. They protested. There was widespread communal fighting, including ethnic clashes and village feuds, all of which claimed many lives. There was also fighting in the eastern part of the country and riots between the Hausa and Fulani in the northern states. Several journalists were killed while reporting on these communal conflicts. In one instance a journalist was arrested and allegedly tortured by police while covering brutal fighting between members of the two ethnic groups.

Moji grew scared of the profession she loved so much. After her youth service with the Sports Commission, she became unemployed again. An embargo was laid on employment with the introduction of the Structural Adjustment Programme (SAP) by the government. The downturn in the economy had resulted in a high unemployment rate. University graduates paced the streets in search of what to do. Life became very tough and getting a job became almost impossible. Graduates filled hundreds of job applications. The few applications that were honoured by companies were those of relatives of top government officials, those who were introduced to the company by important personnel or a politician in the country, those whose fathers had powerful contacts or those who were ready to sleep around.

Media houses did not help the matter. They were willing to combat unemployment by employing graduates but they were not ready to pay salaries. They blamed the economy for this and gave the graduates the option of either accepting the situation and hoping for the best or rejecting the job.

After a long search Moji got a sales job with a company that sold office equipment. Though the salary was bad, the prospects were good. When sales targets were met commissions were paid, and this helped her a lot. She continued to work as a freelance journalist, contributing to various newspapers and journals. She discovered a lot of company executives who were her clients expected to either date or sleep with her if she wanted them to make large orders. She began to feel discouraged again. She tried to figure out a solution to the problem but she couldn't.

A year later, Moji set up a company with one of her closest childhood friends, Agatha. Her sales job had served as an eye opener, opening doors to necessary and meaningful contacts. Agatha and Moji were determined to make it, no matter how difficult things appeared to be. With their contacts, they got contracts from the government and big establishments. The market was very tough, but with time, they broke even. The market was flooded with young graduates who also wanted these contracts for their families. Moji and Agatha learnt it was no longer a matter of those who had the ability, but those who had the right contacts – irrespective of whether the person was literate or not. There was money but the leaders of the country made sure it only circulated within certain pockets. Soon there was a change over in the government. The corruption level in the country rose even higher. Moji and Agatha struggled on. Their business became good and promising. The evolution of new generation banks in Nigeria helped. They took the bull by the horns and explored the opportunities they could get from these banks. They got contracts and made good money. But their dream was short lived. Again the unstable economy bit hard and business became very slow for them. No more opportunities presented themselves. They became idle for months. After many months, another idea came to Moji. She put the little resources she had together and set up a fashion shop in the mainland area of Lagos. The fashion shop had three sections, which served the low-income earners, the middle class and the rich. Moji sold clothes for these classes of people. Her designs for the rich were very exclusive and classy. The section for the middle class had a variety of ranges of designs. The fashion shop boomed and within months Moji arranged for a bigger and better premises in a better location. She got the premises from the previous owner, who had purchased it from the Lagos Island local government. She gave the shop a better design and got some publicity. She acquired more customers. The shop boomed. A new minister for works and housing came into power. He wasn't pleased with the location of many shops. He gave orders for a mass demolition of illegal shops and houses. He also claimed certain lands, houses and shops in Lagos Island belonged to the federal government and not the state's local government. He swung into action and, without any notice, confiscated lands, houses and shops. Moji's shop was one of those to be knocked down.

Moji watched as her shop was demolished. The bulldozer moved into action, raising its dreadful jaw. She watched as it reduced to rubble a business she had spent a fortune to build. She watched as her only source of income, her last hope and all she depended on was crushed.

Rumours went round that the minister wanted the land for his own use, to erect a new building on it.

Moji was reduced to a nervous wreck. She wept for days and ran to her friends for help and assistance. The friends she trusted and believed in gave her the shock of her life. Nobody was willing to help. All the connections she thought she had made turned out to be just shallow and empty.

No compensation was given to anyone. Homes were ruined, people were rendered homeless and years of investment and struggle went down the drain in one day. The government made no provision for those who were affected. Moji found herself going back into the unemployment market. After many weeks, she went back to her friend Agatha.

The hunt for contracts for her and Agatha began again. They struggled for many months. They ran into an old contact and things changed for them. They got contracts worth millions of Naira from the state government. They needed funds for the contracts. They got loans to execute the contracts, with the promise that all contractors would be paid later by the government. But nothing happened when the time came for them to be paid. They panicked. The military in power handed over to a civilian government. There was no mention of those who were owed money. The new government laid an embargo on payment of debts acquired by the old government. A particular governor was quoted as having privately said, 'I did not come here to pay debts. I came to execute my job.' He argued that if he paid the debts owed by the old regime with the money he had in the coffers, there would be nothing left for his state.

Moji, Agatha and many others waited patiently for years, praying for the best. Nothing happened. No news was heard. Nothing was said. Another military ruler came into power with the Third Republic, but nothing was mentioned about the debt owed to hundreds of people by the old regime. Life became tough for Moji. She relied on her friends for food. Her parents were also affected.

Moji had accumulated a lot of debt over the years. The bulk of it was what she had used in executing the contract. Her debtors became very difficult with her. They chased her around for their money, not caring what the government had done to her. They had also been affected in one way or another by the state of the economy. Their businesses had gone down the drain and they needed money to survive. The middle class had vanished. A lot of people had been reduced to begging for clothes, food and money to survive.

Depression set in. Moji lived from hand to mouth. She regretted leaving England after her higher diploma. For weeks, she wept, not knowing where the next meal would come from. Her boyfriend ditched her. He not only cheated and deceived her, but the moment he realised she was broke and her business was no longer booming, he also became cold, distant and unfriendly, giving all sorts of feeble excuses for his behaviour. Moji was devastated to be abandoned at such a time. He broke her heart. She was in her late thirties with no husband, no children and nothing to show for all the years of hard work she had put into her life. But despite all this, her belief in God was strong. She was positive He would grant her heart's desires. She just needed to be patient. Days turned into weeks and weeks into months. The situation remained the same.

Moji continued to maintain contact with her friends in London. Over the years, most of them had made progress and settled there with promising futures. The majority of them had properties at home and abroad. For another couple of years Moji relied on friends. They sent money to her regularly. She deprived herself of so many things and only spent money on what was absolutely necessary for her to survive. With a lot of effort and strong backing from her friends, Moji made her way back to London. She believed it was the only way out.

Gradually Moji began to get on her feet again in London. It was tough because she had no money and no valid papers. She found it difficult to do menial jobs but, with no choice left, she applied for jobs she regarded as dirty and low. She took the offers she got because she had made up her mind not to go back to Nigeria. She updated herself on what was going on in Nigeria. She was eager to know if there was any hope for her to get her money from the government and if there was anything new and promising for journalists. But there was no mention of the money hundreds of people were owed by the government. In 1999, military rule ended with a presidential election.

A new civilian government was installed. Expectations of Nigerians all over the world ran high that the dark days of repression were finally over. Nigerian citizens looked at the new regime as their last hope, even though foreign observers concluded the transition to civilian rule was hardly built on a strong foundation of democracy and human rights. Although a new constitution was promulgated, the media was offered no specific protection. A great number of repressive military decrees that had been there for years remained in force, and, although the number of human-rights abuses decreased significantly during the transition to civilian rule, attacks on the press continued, though on a smaller scale. Copies of any editions of papers that carried headlines describing corruption under the former regime were seized. The lives of journalists were threatened as the attack on the press continued.

Moji remained in England. She constantly ran from the law because she had no papers. She panicked at the sight of any policeman she saw and got more depressed. Even though she felt comfortable staying with Yemi, she couldn't continue to be a burden. She continued to work, saving as much as she could. Then she met Ola. Though she wasn't ready for any commitment, she became pregnant. A part of her was happy; a part wasn't. Her relationship didn't work. Accepting her fate as a single mother, Moji moved on with her life. She continued to work hard. She took up an extra job. She needed to save and she wanted the best for her baby.

One beautiful morning in 1999, as Moji relaxed on her bed trying to enjoy her day off work, a new chapter opened in her life. Yemi had an idea. Moji listened quietly to what she had to say. There seemed to be a way out at last.

Moji was glad to learn she could start a new life in Ireland where she could practise her profession with ease. She was assured there was no harassment of foreigners by the police. The country had hopes for people like her.

It took Moji some time to get herself together and re-plan her future. She believed everything in life was a risk, so she decided take a bold step into the future.

The night before she left for Ireland, Moji sat up in bed reflecting on her life. She wasn't sure of what to expect and the more she thought about it she more confused she got. She put her trust in God, with a strong belief that a blessing in disguise awaited her in Ireland.

As Moji lifted up her hands in prayer she couldn't stop the tears that flowed freely down her cheeks. She prayed for her new home to bring her joy and happiness with the hope that it would be a society with values, free of corruption and good to live in.

References

For country profiles

www.sierraleone.com

www.fbi.com

www.zimbabwe.com

www.nigeria.com

www.nigeriabusinessinfo.com

www.africa.com

AKIDWA Subscription Form

Name _____

Address _____

_____

_____ Phone no _____

1 copy €10

No of copies required

Postage within Ireland €

Postage outside Ireland €

Send a cheque or postal order made payable to:
'AKIDWA' (African Women's Network),
9c Abbey Street
Dublin Central Mission,
Dublin 1, Ireland

AKIDWA Membership Form

Name _____

Address _____

_____

Home Phone _____ Work Phone _____

Membership costs

☐ Group Membership €50 (annually)

☐ Individual €35 (annually)

☐ Supporters €35 (annually)

Please pay AKIDWA annually, starting on ____/____/____

I would like to join the membership of AKIDwA's team on:-
(please tick one or more boxes)

☐ Education/Training Programme

☐ Women/Gender issues

☐ Advocacy/Lobbying

☐ Social/Fundraising activities

☐ General help

☐ Other (specify) _____

For more information email akidwa@eircom.net or call Salome on 00353-87-4150906.